HELP! I'VE BEEN SUED!

TEN STEPS TO AVOID DISASTER

ALICIA I. DEARN, ESQ.

ACID SQUIRREL MEDIA LLC

Published by Fitz & Ferd Ltd. dba Acid Squirrel Media LLC. The names "Fitz & Ferd" and "Acid Squirrel Media" and their logos are trademarks of Acid Squirrel Media LLC.

Print ISBN: 978-1-965282-06-9

Ebook ISBN: 978-1-965282-05-2

https://acidsquirrelmedia.com

DISCLAIMER

This book is for general educational purposes only. It does not constitute legal advice and does not create an attorney-client relationship. Laws vary by jurisdiction, change over time, and may have changed since this book was written. The information in this book reflects the general law of the United States of America. The laws of other jurisdictions may vary.

The information in this book reflects the law as generally understood as of 2026 and may not reflect current developments. No warranty is made regarding the accuracy, completeness, or currency of the information contained herein.

This book is not a substitute for the advice of a licensed attorney. Every legal situation is different, and readers should consult a qualified attorney regarding their specific circumstances before taking any action.

The author and publisher shall not be liable for any loss, damage, or other consequence arising from the use of or reliance on the information in this book.

CONTENTS

INTRODUCTION

Help! I've Been Sued!

You have just had a visit from a process server. A lawsuit is sitting on your desk.

The quiet buzz of the office around you fades. You no longer notice the emails popping up in the corner of your computer screen or the flashing light on your phone. You do not see the pictures of your family on your desk. You do not notice your employees and co-workers walking by your cracked door, stealing quick, curious glances at you.

Your head is in your hands as you stare at the half-inch stack of paper. The writing is tiny legalese and makes about as much sense as a novel written in Pig Latin. But all you can see is your name and the plaintiff's name in big letters at the top. Anger rises in your chest and clenches like a fist around your throat. The angry fist chokes out the curses you are mentally heaping on the plaintiff.

But even as your outrage swells heavily in your chest, fear begins to roil and churn in your stomach. Soon your mind is racing. What does this mean? What will be taken from you? What is at stake?

How long will this take? How much will it cost? Is life, as you know it, ruined?

What should you do? Should you call the plaintiff and ask why they sued you? Should you delete emails and throwing away files? Should you cut off relationships with friends, family, or employees who may be witnesses? Should you throw the lawsuit in the trash and pretend you never received it? Should you put all your money in an offshore bank account? Should you file for bankruptcy and give your house to your kids?

STOP. Do not do *any of those things*.

Who This Book Is For?

This book is for anyone who has recently been served with a civil lawsuit in the United States—individuals, small business owners, corporate officers, non-profit board members, employers, or anyone else who suddenly finds themselves on the wrong end of a summons. It is also for anyone who suspects a lawsuit may come and wants to be prepared when it arrives.

You do not need a legal background to use this book. You do not need to understand the court system, know legal terminology, or have any prior experience with litigation. What you need is the willingness to follow ten concrete steps that will protect you, preserve your options, and position you to defend yourself effectively.

I wrote this book because I have spent over two decades and a thousand cases cleaning up the aftermath of what happens when defendants do not know these steps. Good people—smart, capable, successful people—make catastrophic mistakes in the first days and weeks after being served. They destroyed evidence without knowing that it was evidence. They missed deadlines that handed their opponents an automatic victory. They forgot about insurance policies that would've paid for their entire defense. They hired the wrong lawyer, made the wrong financial moves, or misunderstood the economics of litigation in ways that cost them far more than the lawsuit itself ever should have.

None of those disasters had to happen. That is what this book helps you prevent.

What These Ten Steps Will Do For You?

The ten steps in this book are not ten things to do in the first hour. They are ten categories of disaster that defendants actually experience, and ten ways to avoid them.

The first five steps are immediate triage. Think of them as a tourniquet: actions you can and should take before you have even hired a lawyer, to stop the bleeding before you rush to the hospital. You still need to get to the hospital. But a tourniquet applied correctly in the first few minutes can make the difference between a survivable injury and a fatal one.

- Step 1 identifies who you can safely talk to before the lawsuit creates witnesses out of everyone around you.

- Step 2 tells you to stop destroying evidence immediately, before a routine IT purge or a Friday shredding service turns a defensible case into a five- or six-figure loss.

- Step 3 teaches you how to find your response deadline and write it down, because missing it hands your opponent an automatic win before the fight even starts.

- Step 4 explains how to locate your insurance policies and tender the lawsuit, because there may already be someone contractually obligated to pay for your defense, and they will not do it unless you ask.

- Step 5 asks you to write down everything you remember while it is fresh, in a form that is protected from disclosure, because your memory will degrade under the pressure of litigation and your lawyer needs the truth before the other side distorts it.

The second five steps take you further. Once the immediate crisis is stabilized, you face an important set of decisions—ones that will shape the next one to three years of your life and determine whether this lawsuit ends as a manageable problem or a financial catastrophe.

- Step 6 educates you on the structure of a lawsuit so you know what you are facing, how long it will take, and what it will cost, because unrealistic expectations are one of the most common causes of poor decisions in litigation.

- Step 7 walks you through how to find, evaluate, and hire the right lawyer—not just any lawyer, but the one who is right for *your* case, *your* goals, and *your* circumstances. This is the longest step in the book because it is the most consequential decision you will make.

- Step 8 helps you understand your damages exposure and

build a litigation budget, so you can make rational decisions about how aggressively to fight and when to consider resolution.

- Step 9 addresses early settlement: what it means, what it costs, when it makes sense, and how to approach it strategically rather than emotionally.

- Step 10 warns you about the financial mistakes that defendants sometimes make after a lawsuit is filed, including fraudulent transfers, asset intermingling, impulsive bankruptcy filings, and other moves that can transform a civil dispute into something much worse.

The book closes with a bonus chapter on the risks of relying on AI instead of counsel—a danger that did not exist when I wrote the first edition of this book just over a decade ago, and that is now one of the most common mistakes defendants make.

A Note on How to Use This Book

Each chapter ends with an executive summary: a short list of action items that captures the essential points. **If you are reading this in a state of acute panic, go to the executive summaries first**. They will tell you what to do right now. Then come back and read the chapters when you are calmer and ready to understand the reasoning behind each step.

The reasoning matters. Not because you need to become a lawyer, but because understanding why these steps are important makes you more likely to follow them and more capable of having an informed conversation with the lawyer you are about to hire. A defendant who understands the stakes is a defendant who makes better decisions. And better decisions, made early, are worth more than excellent lawyering applied to a mess that did not have to happen.

Before You Turn the Page

In my practice, I have seen defendants who followed every one of these steps and came through their lawsuits intact—financially, professionally, and personally. I have also seen defendants who ignored them, and I have had to deal with the aftermath of these avoidable mistakes.

The difference is rarely intelligence or resources. It is information applied at the right moment.

You have the information now.

INTRODUCTION EXECUTIVE SUMMARY

The Ten Steps to Avoid Disaster

1. Take a deep breath and identify your Circle of Trust
2. Stop all routine destruction of documents and back up your data
3. Calculate the deadline to answer the lawsuit and write it down
4. Dig out your insurance policies and tender the lawsuit for coverage
5. Make a timeline of events and identify documents and witnesses
6. Educate yourself on the basic lawsuit process

7. Hire the right lawyer

8. Analyze your damages exposure and build a defense budget

9. Consider early settlement

10. Plan your finances, upcoming transactions, and assets carefully

Bonus Chapter: The Risks of Relying on AI Instead of Counsel

STEP 1

TAKE A DEEP BREATH AND IDENTIFY YOUR CIRCLE OF TRUST

Take a Deep Breath

Being sued is like someone coming up to you and punching you right in the nose. It's openly, nakedly aggressive. It's a threat. Your nervous system will react accordingly.

I've litigated over a thousand cases, so my reaction to most of them is an eye-roll. But that's not the reaction by any of my clients.

So the very first piece of advice I have for you is the same advice that opens *The Hitchhiker's Guide to the Galaxy*: Don't Panic. I promise the world is not about to collapse on your head.

Take a deep breath and calm your natural parasympathetic reaction.

Maybe take a few more.

Feeling a little calmer? Good.

How to Get Your Mom Subpoenaed

Can you imagine your mother being called to testify against you? I've seen it. I've defended against it. One client spoke to her mother about several issues in the lawsuit. Those conversations counted as admissions by the defendant, and her mother was called to the stand to recount them.

Even if your mom is completely on your side, if she remembers you saying something different from what you remembered and testified—well, the jury is going to believe your mom. You won't be able to correct her before testifying. If you try, it'll be subject to examination (which will make you look bad), and could be considered witness tampering.

Neither you nor your mom wants this experience.

So how does this happen? Simply, it is normal to be angry or anxious when you are served with a lawsuit. And your first instinct will be to seek relief from that anxiety, which most people do by leaning on the comfort, advice, and sympathy of other people. This instinct, however understandable, creates a bunch of witnesses out of your friends, family, and employees.

DO NOT DO THIS.

You should not assume that the lawyer who filed the lawsuit against you is nice, reasonable, or honorable. They *may* be. But they also may lack the human decency to leave your mom out of it. That's why you should assume your loved ones could get subpoenaed. In my practice, I have seen romantic partners, exes, parents, friends, employees, business partners, accountants, professional colleagues, social media, teachers, and even children get subpoenaed.

What Is the Circle of Trust, and Why Does It Matter?

While you go through this process, you will, in fact, need emotional support from your people. So I am not telling you that you will never be able to discuss this with your mom. But she should not be your first phone call.

Before you say a word to anyone—before you pick up the phone, before you fire off an email, before you call an emergency staff meeting, and (*for the love of God*) before you post on social media or ask ChatGPT what you should do—you need to stop and identify your Circle of Trust. Not just based on how tight you are with someone, but also based on legal privileges.

Most people, and even AI, can be subpoenaed and forced to testify to anything you tell them. Who can't be? Your lawful spouse, your lawyer, your doctor and therapist, and your priest.

The Circle of Trust is your need-to-know group and, ideally, should involve a lawyer immediately. Conversations you have with lawyers (regardless of whether they end up representing you) are the most protected. The attorney-client privilege is inviolable to encourage candor. A lawyer is in the best position to tell you the truth about what you're facing and to help you navigate it. Lawyers can advise you on who you can speak to about the case and what you may say, so you can control your blood pressure.

Everyone else—no matter how close, how loyal, or how well-meaning—waits.

> **POINTER**: This comes up a lot and bears mentioning: Your romantic partner can be subpoenaed. Spousal and marital privileges exist (they vary significantly by state and are not as absolute as attorney-client privileges). But unless you are legally married, they do not apply. You may have lived together for decades and have children together. That won't count for a hill of beans for the spousal privilege.

Besides the harassment of your social circle being subjected to subpoena, it can have a deleterious impact on your case. Witnesses who learn about a lawsuit before your lawyer has assessed them, prepared them, or taken their spontaneous statements, are witnesses who may give inconsistent testimony, or—in the worst cases—compare notes with other witnesses, revise their memories, and decide that they have their own grievances.

That last possibility is not hypothetical. I have seen it happen countless times in employee lawsuits against smaller employers. A defendant employer, blindsided and hurt by the allegations, tells other employees in their office, only to see other employees feed information to the plaintiff. Or perhaps the employer later has to fire some poor performers, and they, knowing about the lawsuit, join it as plaintiffs. A single lawsuit becomes three. A manageable problem becomes a catastrophe, all before the defense attorney was ever hired. It is better for your attorney to root out and address grievances without litigation, which means they must control communication around the lawsuit.

> **POINTER**: Anything you post online, whether it be on social media or to AI, whether it be to vent or to get advice, is discoverable. For that matter, your own notes and journals are discoverable. Nothing you write, post, or search is confidential or privileged.

It is commonplace now for lawyers to immediately subpoena social media and AI and browser histories for your posts. No one on Facebook is an adequate substitute for a lawyer. That's doubly the case for ChatGPT. AI has its uses, but it lacks the experience, skills, nuance, and judgment of a lawyer.

Who Belongs in the Circle?

The Circle of Trust is not a fixed list. It will vary depending on whether you are an individual defendant, a small business owner, a corporate officer, etcetera. But as a general rule, your Circle of Trust in the first days after service includes:

- *You*. Keep your own counsel. This is an under-appreciated skill. Although the Fifth Amendment (the right to remain silent) does not apply to civil lawsuits, it is still your first and best line of defense. You don't need to volunteer information before the case ever gets to court.

- *Your lawyer*. Not everyone has a lawyer on-call. But finding a lawyer should be at the very top of your list if you get sued.

- *Your legal spouse*. If you have a legal spouse or domestic partner, check your jurisdiction's rules on the privilege. A romantic partner can be a great emotional support. Even if you are not protected by legal privileges, your romantic partner may need to know if the lawsuit involves shared assets, finances, or anything that will directly affect your household and emotional well-being. A lawyer will be able to advise you on the finer points of what you can and should share with your significant other.

- *Your business partners and senior management*. If the lawsuit involves your business, your legal business partners (as in, those who own a part of the business, not just people you mutually work with) have a right to know about it. Your senior management staff may also need to know to the extent that it impacts their operational responsibilities. For example, in Step 2, you will need to preserve evidence. That may require the involvement of IT, Human Resources, or others in management. Even still, while they may be told to put a litigation hold on evidence, you do not need to tell them everything about the suit.

- *Your insurance broker*. We will cover this in detail in Step 4, but your broker needs to know quickly because there are deadlines and duties involved in tendering a claim. Your broker is a professional with confidentiality obligations and a financial incentive to handle this properly. And again, you do not need to tell them everything about the suit.

- *Your therapist, psychiatrist, doctor, or religious leader*. Getting sued is stressful. You don't have to navigate your anxiety alone. If you need spiritual or emotional counsel or anti-anxiety medication, there is no shame in seeking it. Medical and religious privileges are essentially universal in the United States. If you have questions about them, ask your lawyer.

That is likely it—the only people you can talk to at first. I know that feels austere. I know that your instinct is that more people knowing means more people helping. But in the first days of a lawsuit, more people knowing almost always means more problems later.

I'm a Business. What About My Team?

I get asked this question in some form at nearly every initial consultation: What do I tell my team, colleagues, partners, and employees? And the answer is: Nothing yet; not without a plan that includes me first.

Here's why: When employees, business partners, and even professional colleagues learn that someone has been sued, they react. Some react with loyalty. Some react with fear. Some react with curiosity. And some—sometimes ones you would never expect—react by quietly calling a lawyer of their own or leveraging against you. The announcement of a lawsuit can function like a starter pistol for people who have grievances or see a competitive advantage. That someone else took legal action makes it feel safe, validated, or profitable for them to do the same. Sometimes it is something as irritating as customers delaying payment on their bills because they think you might be drained of resources to collect (or fold the business) and they can avoid payment.

Beyond that, there is a tactical concern. If employees or partners are potential witnesses—and in most business litigation, they will be—you want your lawyer to take down their spontaneous, uncoached recollections before they have had time to discuss the facts with each other, revise their memories, or align their stories. Once people talk, you lose the freshness of their individual recollections. That freshness is often where the truth lives, and your lawyer needs access to it.

What About Friends and Family?

Even though I just told you several times that friends and family can be turned into witnesses, it is not realistic for me to tell you that you cannot talk to your spouse or your closest confidants about your stress. You are a human being dealing with a frightening situation, and emotional support matters. You're going to do it, and I don't want you to lie to your lawyer about it when you do.

But I am going to give you some practical guidance about what those conversations should and should not include.

> **POINTER**: Here's a little script for you. "Hey mom. I'm very stressed because John Doe sued my company for wrongful termination. My lawyer says I can't tell you any of the details. But I'm allowed to

share with you how upset I feel, and that I'm worried about what it'll cost to defend. Send cookies."

Do not share the details of the lawsuit with people outside your Circle of Trust. "Details" includes: the allegations; who was involved; what you recall; your analysis of the case; what you remember about the incident; what you told your lawyer or what your lawyer told you; your defense strategy; or your desire for violent revenge.

Again, anything you say to people who aren't protected by privilege (lawyer, priest, doctor, legal spouse) is discoverable. Privilege does not extend to conversations with friends, family, colleagues, or AI software and strangers on the internet.

Technically, if you tell your mom you're upset about being sued, that is also discoverable. It's just that the opposing lawyer is unlikely to care about that because it is rarely relevant evidence to the lawsuit. So if this gets discovered, it is unlikely to result in a trial subpoena to your mom.

Keep the details inside the Circle of Trust for now. Keep the emotional processing as general as possible outside it. You can tell your best friend you are going through a difficult legal situation without handing them a roadmap to your defense strategy.

Can I Contact the Plaintiff or Their Lawyer?

It's still a free country, but please don't do that.

Recall what I told you about the other side not being presumptively nice or reasonable? If you call them, you are exceedingly unlikely to resolve the dispute. If the dispute were that easy to resolve, they wouldn't have sued you in the first place. Calling the other side is more likely to have one or more of several consequences: they get admissions out of you that are detrimental to your defense later; they pressure you into agreeing to a settlement that is against your interest; they cause you compounding emotional distress and frustration; and/or they accuse you of witness tampering by saying you are pressuring the plaintiff.

There's very little upside and the potential for a lot of downside. You're better off following the Ten Steps in this book instead.

STEP 1 EXECUTIVE SUMMARY

- Immediately stop all routine destruction of documents and back up your data.

- Take a deep breath (or several). Don't panic.

- Resist the urge to tell anyone about the lawsuit until you have thought carefully about who needs to know right away.

- Identify your Circle of Trust: yourself; your lawyer; your spouse or partner; your most essential business partners and managers; your insurance broker; and your mental health, physical health, and spiritual health practitioners.

- Do not seek advice online, whether on social media, browser searches, or AI tools like ChatGPT. Anything you put in writing, and any conversations you have, about the lawsuit can and will be discovered.

- Do not announce the lawsuit to employees, staff, or the broader organization until you have legal guidance.
- Keep emotional support conversations with your friends and family generic. Share your stress, not your strategy.
- Do not contact the plaintiff, the plaintiff's attorney, or anyone else connected to the lawsuit without your attorney present.

STEP 2

Immediately stop all routine destruction of documents and back up your data.

The lawsuit is in your hands. Your mind is already racing through everything you need to do: find a lawyer, notify your partner, figure out what this is going to cost you. In the middle of all that noise, your IT manager's quarterly notification pops up on your calendar. It's time for the quarterly server purge. Your assistant reminds you that the shredding service is coming on Friday and asks if they can take the pile of paper under the window. Your telephone company sends a text inviting you to upgrade all your company phones.

NOPE. Time to stop *all of that*.

Nothing gets deleted. Nothing gets shredded. Nothing gets wiped, purged, archived off-site, or thrown in the trash. No hardware gets replaced. Not today. Not Friday. Not until your lawyer tells you otherwise. Because the moment you were served with that lawsuit, the rules changed. And what feels like routine housekeeping can now get you sanctioned, fined, or worse.

How a Cell Phone Upgrade Lost The Whole Case

I have my clients preserve evidence, so I'm going to tell you a story about how I once used the failure to preserve to sink my opponent's entire case. In that case, the plaintiff alleged that my client had said something incriminating to her via text. My client said it wasn't true. The plaintiff provided "print offs" of the text messages but not the original messages themselves. My client no longer had any of the text messages, but said the produced messages were fabricated and out of context.

At the deposition, I learned that the print-offs were transcriptions of the text messages that the plaintiff had given orally to her lawyer's paralegal, making it hearsay and unauthenticated evidence. I subpoenaed the plaintiff's cell phone records and demanded to inspect the phone with a forensic expert.

The plaintiff, however, said she'd "lost" the phone before admitting she'd turned it in to her cell phone company for an upgrade and that the alleged text messages hadn't transferred to the new device. Worse, she had done this after the lawsuit had been filed—which means she clearly had the duty to preserve the evidence already. In contrast, my client had deleted text messages with the plaintiff long before he ever had reason to suspect a lawsuit.

Long story short, I had the alleged text messages excluded because the plaintiff had the duty to preserve the evidence once she knew the legal dispute existed, and she failed. Soon after, she dropped the case to avoid sanctions and legal costs.

That's what happens if you don't preserve evidence. That's why your lawyer will usually start with giving you instructions for a

Litigation Hold.

What Is a Litigation Hold?

Once you are on notice that you have a legal dispute, you are required by law to preserve all evidence that is potentially relevant to the case. This obligation does not begin when you hire a lawyer. It does not begin when you file your answer. It begins the moment you have any reason to expect a legal dispute (such as a threat from the plaintiff, a complaint to a government agency, a demand letter, or service of a lawsuit).

This duty to preserve evidence is called a litigation hold, and it means exactly what it sounds like: you hold everything. You do not yet know what is relevant and what is not. That determination requires legal expertise you do not have right now, and your lawyer will help you refine it later. For now, the safest and smartest posture is to preserve everything and sort it out with counsel.

At a minimum, a litigation hold covers:

- Printed documents of any kind
- Handwritten notes, including Post-its, scratch paper, and napkin scribbles
- Calendars, journals, and diaries
- Email, including sent items, drafts, and deleted folders
- Letters and envelopes
- Physical evidence such as vehicles, products, equipment,

or anything else connected to the dispute

- Photographs, video, and audio recordings
- Hard drives, servers, and backup systems
- Cell phones and tablets
- Computers, laptops, and any personal devices used for work
- Cloud storage and third-party platforms, such as Dropbox, Google Drive, iCloud, etc.
- Accounting databases and financial records
- Text messages and messaging apps, like WhatsApp, Messenger, Teams, Slack, and others
- Social media accounts
- Browser and AI search histories
- Voicemails and itemized phone bills with call logs

That list is longer than most people expect. And it is not exhaustive. If you are looking at something and wondering whether it counts, the answer is to preserve it and let your lawyer decide later.

What Do I Actually Have to Do Right Now?

You do not need to understand the full scope of your discovery obligations today. What you need to do today is hit pause on your normal routines and get everything backed up.

Start with your electronic systems. Back up all of your electronic data immediately—hard drives, servers, websites, cloud storage, and email. Stop any routine deletion of old backups or old emails. If your company runs automated purges on a schedule, suspend them now. Back up and preserve security footage, images, and videos, as this type of media gets overwritten quickly.

> **POINTER**: Employees can delete emails from their own inboxes, but in most business systems, you can preserve and archive emails without their knowledge. Your IT team or managed services provider can set this up quickly. Do it before anyone knows what is happening.

Next, address your physical documents. Stop shredding. Stop the routine trash. Stop the Friday document destruction service. Everything that touches the subject matter of the lawsuit or the people involved stays put. (You can still throw away your old coffee grounds and the lunch trash *because Bob won't stop eating a daily can of sardines.*)

Finally, put a hold on equipment upgrades (especially mobile devices and computers). If other physical items are involved, like vehicles or products, set those aside as well. The gold standard is keeping anything that might be evidence locked up where it cannot be tampered with until after your lawyer has advised you on it.

Are you actually going to need all of this stuff? No. Most of what you preserve will never be looked at twice. But you should not try to judge for yourself what is important at this stage. Knowing what comprises relevant, discoverable, or admissible evidence is a specialized skill that lawyers spend years developing. You do not have years. Just preserve it all and let your lawyer sort it out. (Plus, your lawyer may choose to dump it all on the plaintiffs and make them sort through it. That's a legitimate and occasionally amusing strategy.)

Why Should I Do This?

You should do this because the consequences of not doing it are severe. Destruction of evidence—whether purposeful, accidental, or routine purging—can be catastrophic to your case. Once you are on notice of a legal dispute, the obligation to preserve is absolute, with serious penalties if you fail.

Here are some examples of what that looks like in practice, because the case law on this is both instructive and unforgiving.

- In *Knickerbocker v. Corinthian Colleges*, 298 F.R.D . 670 (W.D. Wash. 2014), Corinthian Colleges was fined $25,000 for failing to suspend an automated IT policy that purged terminated employees' email accounts after 30 days. No ill intent required—just sloppiness.

- The consequences escalate dramatically when omissions look like a pattern. In *Sentis Group, Inc. v. Shell Oil Co.*, 763 F.3d 919 (8th Cir. 2014), a plaintiff had their entire case thrown out. A failure to preserve data held by their outside accountant contributed to this result. The court did not care that the accountant was not their employee.

- Even when you reverse the worst-case scenario on appeal, the litigation costs of a preservation failure are massive. In *Cowan Systems, LLC v. Collier*, 361 Ga. App. 823 (2021), a trucking company installed electronic data recorders on its fleet but never built an operational habit of actually downloading and saving the records. When an accident led to a lawsuit, the data was long gone. While the appellate court ultimately spared the company from a severe adverse jury instruction, the company still faced lesser sanctions and a costly appellate battle entirely because it failed to establish good data habits from day one.

- And then there is *Parlux Fragrances v. S. Carter Enterprises,* 69 Misc.3d 1209(A) (N.Y. Sup. Ct. 2020)—better known as the Jay-Z cologne lawsuit. The court imposed severe sanctions and a sweeping adverse inference instruction against the defendants because they wiped a year's worth of emails during a routine January clean-up, completely ignoring a demand letter sent by the plaintiff the previous July, even though it was long before the lawsuit was filed.

The adverse inference sanction (as illustrated in *Parlux Fra-*

grances) is worth understanding because it is one of the most damaging things a court can do to your case short of dismissing it outright. An adverse inference instruction tells the jury that because you destroyed evidence, they are required to presume the evidence was unfavorable to you. Your lawyer cannot argue around it. The jury knows that something was destroyed, and the legal instruction tells them they must assume the worst. That instruction alone can determine the outcome.

The worst-case scenario for spoliation—the legal term for the destruction of evidence—is that the court strikes your entire side of the case, bars you from testifying or introducing evidence of your own, and directs judgment for the other side in whatever amount they request. You lose before you even start.

Yeah, Okay. But I'm Not Amazon.

Perhaps you are thinking: those are big companies. Those cases don't apply to me. I'm just an individual. Or, I'm a small business without an IT department.

Sorry. These laws apply to all litigants, large and small. I have dealt with spoliation issues many times in cases involving small businesses and unsophisticated individuals. The court does not grade on a curve for small defendants.

I have been on the wrong side of this equation. I have helped clients recover lost evidence at great expense, manage sanctions motions, and fire employees who destroyed evidence while a lawsuit was pending. Even though I have so far always been able to contain the damage, it was never clean. It added cost and complexity and put an otherwise innocent party in a deeply uncomfortable position.

Won't A Litigation Hold Mean Everyone Will Know I Was Sued?

Given everything I just told you, you may wonder whether you are immediately required to broadcast to your entire business or professional organization that you have been sued and that everyone must stop deleting things. And you may also wonder how that squares with the secrecy I counseled in Step 1.

You don't need to broadcast it yet, and definitely not without a plan. A blanket announcement creates the exact witness contamination problems we discussed in Step 1. Employees who learn about a lawsuit before your lawyer has assessed them may start comparing notes, crafting stories, or quietly calling their own attorneys. You want to avoid that.

The good news is you can suspend your own document destruction routines—and direct your most essential IT and operations people to do the same—without broadcasting the reason. Even for very small businesses, the administrator for your tech systems can control deletion on the server side without your employees ever knowing. You can also back up employee devices and stop shredding without explaining why.

When the time comes to issue a formal litigation hold notice to your broader team, your lawyer will draft it carefully, direct it to the right people, and time it strategically. That notice will tell the relevant personnel exactly what to preserve and how, without unnecessarily alarming the entire organization or tipping off witnesses prematurely.

Until then, keep the Circle of Trust tight, suspend the routines, and back everything up.

A Note on Third Parties

One of the most common and costly mistakes defendants make is assuming that their preservation obligation only extends to their own devices and systems. It does not.

If relevant data exists on the personal cell phone of an employee, a contractor, a vendor, or a business partner, and it is within your reasonable ability to preserve it, you may have an obligation to do so. For example, if your outside accountant has files relevant to the dispute, as in the *Sentis* case, those files are your problem too. You may have to tell those people directly that there is a lawsuit and they must not delete information.

Make sure you preserve the data you're sharing with your contractors and advisors. If any of them are holding data without your ability to back it up, please ask them not to delete or destroy anything, even if it's just a quick email until your lawyer can send out a formal Litigation Hold memorandum.

Flag these issues for your lawyer immediately. The question of whose devices and accounts fall within your Litigation Hold is one of the first things a competent attorney will work through with you. And the sooner you raise it, the better your position.

STEP 2 EXECUTIVE SUMMARY

- Immediately suspend all routine electronic data deletions, scheduled purges, and automated archiving.

- Back up everything: hard drives, servers, cloud storage, email, video and photo storage, and messaging platforms.
- Stop shredding and cancel or postpone any scheduled physical document destruction.
- Preserve all potentially relevant physical evidence: devices, equipment, vehicles, products, or anything connected to the dispute.
- Alert essential IT or operations personnel to pause destruction routines.
- Do not decide what is relevant and what is not. Preserve everything and let your lawyer sort it out.
- Flag any third-party devices or accounts that may contain relevant data, ask them not to delete things not in your power to back up, and raise this with your lawyer immediately.
- Issue a broader Litigation Hold notice that your lawyer prepares and gives you instructions on.

STEP 3

FIND THE DEADLINE TO ANSWER THE LAWSUIT AND WRITE IT DOWN.

The hands-down most common mistake I see by defendants is missing the deadline to respond to the lawsuit. This usually results from administrative errors, lack of money to hire a lawyer, mistaken belief that you can negotiate a resolution with the plaintiff directly, or panic that results in a freeze and sticking the lawsuit in a drawer. Doing nothing—whether out of shock, denial, lack of resources, or the mistaken belief that the lawsuit will somehow go away—always turns out badly.

Usually, it results in a default judgment. A default occurs when you fail to respond, and the court gives the plaintiff an automatic win. To avoid that, you want to calculate the due date and make sure you do not miss it. The clock to calculate the due date starts the moment the process server hands you the lawsuit.

The Seven Million Dollar Problem

Default judgments are not always the end of the story. I've gotten around a bunch of them. But it's an ugly, stressful ride.

A few years ago, inadvertence resulted in a default judgment against a small business to the horrific, life-altering amount of nearly $7,000,000.

It started innocently enough. At the time the lawsuit was served, the business owner had been absent from work due to serious health issues. Her service agent received the lawsuit on her behalf and sent it to her by email through his employee. It went to her junk mail; no one saw it, and the agent didn't follow up.

A few months later, when the service agent received the default judgment, he contacted me. The client had to retain me out-of-pocket. I was able to reverse the judgment, secure insurance defense counsel, and preserve evidence before this problem put the business and its owners into bankruptcy. But that process cost them thousands in extra legal fees and *months* of stress when the owner was already dealing with serious health concerns. It also impacted settlement discussions and litigation posture by the opposing side for two years, making the case difficult to resolve.

Stupid mistake. Big consequences. Mind your deadline.

Where Do I Find My Deadline?

The lawsuit you were handed is a packet of documents. The first page (usually)—the one printed in what looks like six-point font and filled with language that reads like it was written for someone other than you—is the summons. It is the most important page in the packet, and it is the first thing you need to read carefully.

The summons will tell you two critical things: the date you were served, and the number of days you have to respond. Find both of those pieces of information right now. Write them down.

Then do the math: add the number of specified days to the date of service, and that is your deadline. The best way to do this is to use a calendar and literally count the days between the service date and the deadline.

> **POINTER**: Always calculate the date twice. Do it by hand and then check your math using the Date Calculator at timeanddate.com. I've been practicing law for over twenty years, and I still always do a double calculation on court dates. I have that website bookmarked.

Now that you have your deadline, write it down somewhere you will not lose it or forget it. Put it in your phone. Put it on a sticky note on your monitor. Set a reminder on your calendar or reminders apps, with extra time so you don't forget until the day it is due.

Do whatever it takes to make sure that date does not slip past you.

Your deadline to respond is usually between 21 and 30 days from service. However, I have seen it as short as 5 days and as long as 60 days, depending on the court, the type of case, and the jurisdiction. Federal court deadlines differ from state court deadlines. Some specialized courts—small claims, landlord-tenant, administrative tribunals—have their own rules entirely. Do not assume. **Read the summons**.

One important note on service date: it is the day the process server physically handed you the documents, not the day you read them, not the day you called your business partner or hired a lawyer, and not the day you feel emotionally ready to take it seriously. If you left the packet sitting on your desk for three days before opening it, you have lost three days. The clock does not pause until you're ready.

If the lawsuit was served to you some other way (mail being the most common), this may impact how much time you have to respond by adding days. Calculate the date with the shortest time stated by the summons and let a lawyer determine whether you have more time. **Do not try to interpret the rules yourself**.

> **POINTER**: Contact and hire lawyers with enough time that you can engage one and have them complete the paperwork on time to meet the deadline. The minimum time you need between consultation, retainer, and filing of a response is several days.

In Case I Wasn't Clear: Read the Summons. Calculate the Date. Do Not Interpret the Law.

Here is where I need to issue a firm caution. Reading the summons to find your deadline is something you can and must do yourself, immediately. But that is where your self-directed legal analysis should stop.

The summons and complaint are legal documents drafted by an opposing attorney whose job is to frame the facts and law in the way most favorable to the plaintiff. What they allege, how they characterize your conduct, and what they claim you owe are not neutral statements of fact. They are the opening argument of someone who wants to take something from you.

You are going to read the complaint (sometimes called a petition) and have feelings about it. You may think it is full of lies. You may think it mischaracterizes everything that happened. You may think parts of it are actually true, and those parts will terrify you. You may see claims you do not recognize and assume they are nonsense. You may encounter legal terms that you do not understand.

Do not do any of this alone, and do not act on any conclusions you reach from reading it yourself. Complaints are written in legal shorthand that carries technical meaning invisible to non-lawyers. A claim that sounds absurd to you may be legally viable. A claim that sounds devastating may have a complete defense you are not aware of. The damages number at the top may be a good-faith estimate, an inflated opening position, or a number designed to frighten you into a bad settlement or grab media attention. Sometimes the prayer for relief is based entirely on technical legal requirements that are unrelated to the facts. You cannot tell which one it is without legal training and knowledge of how courts in your jurisdiction handle these claims.

More importantly, the complaint may contain procedural vulnerabilities—defects in how it was filed, claims that do not meet the legal standard, jurisdictional problems, or failures to state a legally recognizable cause of action—that an experienced lawyer can exploit in a motion to dismiss before you ever file an answer. Those opportunities disappear if you miss the deadline or if you file a defective answer on your own that inadvertently waives them. The complaint tells you what you are up against. It does not tell you how to respond to it. That requires a lawyer.

If you focus on all those aspects, you may forget to calculate and calendar the response deadline. Stop! Do not pass Go! Do not interpret the lawsuit before you calculate and calendar that deadline, so you know how long you have to find and retain a lawyer. Do not start panic-calling people and throwing paper at the court. DO NOT STICK IT IN A DRAWER.

Why You Cannot Answer It Yourself

I understand the impulse. The complaint says things that are wrong, and you want to correct them. You are a capable, intelligent person. You can write. How hard can it be?

Very hard. And the consequences of doing it wrong are serious.

I've got another story for you. I had a case where the defendants were cash-poor, and so they hired a paralegal to prepare an answer for them. They filed the answer as self-represented parties. Fortunately, that answer was defective in several ways, and the court rejected it, putting them in default. I say "fortunately" because after that, they hired me. And they had a defense that allowed me to move to dismiss immediately. That defense and dismissal motion would've been waived if the answer had been accepted. Unfortunately, though, I had to contend with a default in addition to my dismissal motion, which added expense.

My point is: this is harder than it looks and why lawyers take years of schooling and a bar exam before they are allowed to do it on your behalf. An answer is not a letter explaining your side of the story. It is a formal legal pleading that must meet certain procedural requirements in responding to the allegations and preserving defenses. Failure to do this right can cut your defense off at the knees, or result in an admission that can be used against you later.

Beyond denying the allegations in the lawsuit, your lawyer will evaluate whether to file a motion to dismiss instead of, or in addition to, an answer. A motion to dismiss challenges the legal sufficiency of the complaint before any factual dispute is litigated. If the complaint has legal defects, a motion to dismiss can end the case early or narrow it significantly. You will not know to look for those defects, and even if you find them, you will not know how to brief them correctly.

An answer also requires you to assert your affirmative defenses—legal defenses that, if not raised correctly in your answer, are permanently waived. There are dozens of potential affirmative defenses depending on your case, and not raising them at the outset means you cannot raise them later. A lawyer knows which ones apply to your situation. You likely do not.

Do not answer the complaint yourself. The money you think you are saving is a fraction of what you will lose if you get it wrong.

What Happens If You Default

A default occurs when you fail to respond to a lawsuit by the deadline. What happens next is that the court assumes you have waived all your denials and defenses by not asserting them, and the other side will automatically win. You cannot say or do anything in the case once a default is entered, other than move to have the default set aside (if that's available).

When a default is entered against you, the plaintiff moves for a default judgment. In most jurisdictions, this is a straightforward process requiring minimal additional showing by the plaintiff. The plaintiff gives the court a short accounting of damages they request, and the court enters judgment for the amount the plaintiff requested—with no examination of whether the claims were meritorious, whether the damages were reasonable, or whether you had a complete defense.

Default judgments are also enforceable immediately. The plaintiff can begin collecting—garnishing wages, levying bank accounts, placing liens on property—as soon as the judgment is entered. Your reputation takes a hit because judgments are public record. Your assets become exposed. And all of this happens before you've had a single opportunity to tell your side of the story.

Even criminals know better than to plead guilty before getting a deal from the prosecution for a lighter sentence. Don't make this mistake! You can usually do better by answering, even if you are on the losing end of the case, because then you have some negotiating power for a settlement, if nothing else. Even if a default judgment is strategically better, this is a risky strategy that requires legal counsel and eyes-wide-open going in.

If You Have Already Defaulted

If you are reading this after a default has already been entered against you, do not close the book. It's not necessarily all over. Defaults can sometimes be set aside, but the standard is demanding and the window is narrow.

I have successfully vacated default judgments many times. But be aware that plaintiffs did not relinquish large judgments willingly. And the longer it takes for you to respond, the harder it is to get the judgment overturned. At some point, it becomes impossible. So if you are in this position, *call a lawyer today*. Not this week. Today. Every day that passes after a default is entered narrows your options and strengthens the plaintiff's position.

Can I Get An Extension on the Deadline?

If you find yourself close to the deadline and without a lawyer, it is often possible to get a brief extension of time to respond. Many opposing lawyers will agree to a short extension as a professional courtesy, particularly if you reach out promptly and explain that you are in the process of retaining counsel. Some courts require extensions be requested by written stipulation or by motion. Some allow the parties to agree without court approval.

> **POINTER**: Do not count on getting an extension. You should not wait until the last minute to look for a lawyer, assuming you'll get an extension. If the other side refuses, you'll be in a bind.

> **POINTER**: Even better, hire a lawyer and let them request the extension (which is usually easy for a lawyer to get). It is still best not to negotiate directly with opposing counsel without your own lawyer involved. An opposing attorney who agrees to an extension may be running out the clock on something, or may attempt to extract concessions first. Try not

to put yourself in that position.

POINTER: Do not assume that settlement discussions will relieve you of the deadline to answer. I see this mistake a lot. Even if you are in active negotiations and the case seems like it'll resolve, until a settlement agreement is signed, court deadlines are in full force.

BONUS POINTER: If the plaintiff suggests a tolling agreement, that may be advisable, but you really do not want to sign anything like that without counsel's advice.

STEP 3 EXECUTIVE SUMMARY

- Find the summons and read it carefully.
- Write down the date you were served. That is when the clock started.
- Find the number of days you have to respond stated in the summons and calculate your deadline. Double check it. Write it down with reminders.
- Read the complaint to understand what you are facing,

but don't interpret the law, evaluate the claims, or draft a response on your own.

- Retain a lawyer with enough time for them to evaluate the case and prepare a proper response.
- Do not answer the complaint yourself. The cost of getting it wrong far exceeds the cost of hiring a lawyer to do it right.
- Do not miss the date to respond, even if you are in negotiations with the other side. That can result in a default judgment.
- If you have already defaulted, call a lawyer today. Time is the one thing you cannot recover.

STEP 4

DIG OUT YOUR INSURANCE POLICIES AND SEND THE LAWSUIT TO YOUR BROKER.

This next step applies whether you are a business or an individual. In a lawsuit, the availability of insurance could be your best friend, and you may be surprised where coverage applies.

Insurance Covers Things You Don't Expect

A few years ago, I was walking my dog across a shopping center parking lot. As we passed a parked car, a forklift dropped its load, resulting in a loud crash. This startled my dog, who jumped and hit a shopping cart sitting next to the car with seventy pounds of terrified fluff. The shopping cart flipped up from the rear and bumped the car it was sitting next to.

After I calmed my dog down, the driver (who was loading their car) demanded my car insurance for alleged damage to their paint job. I said no because I was not driving a car when the accident happened. My car wasn't even there.

Instead, I gave them my business card and took a picture of the damage they claimed (I didn't see any on close inspection). I told them to get a quote for repair, contact me, and we would discuss it. (I would never admit things at the scene of an accident—lawyer training—although I don't think I was negligent here anyway.)

They never called. But if they had, I might've tendered the claim to my homeowners' insurance. Because certain torts (including things like defamation or injuries caused by your dog) can be covered by your homeowners' liability insurance, regardless of whether the injury happened at your home.

Similarly, when my clients are sued, one of the first things I ask them about is all their insurance policies. And I have them tender to those policies even if coverage is a stretch. Because I have repeatedly achieved coverage for suits that surprised the client, and even the broker.

What Does It Actually Cost to Defend a Lawsuit?

Tendering to insurance is a simple move that can save you tens or even hundreds of thousands of dollars—because there may already be someone contractually obligated to pay for your defense. But they won't do it unless you ask first.

Let me give you some numbers, because this step becomes a lot more urgent when you understand what is at stake financially.

The average cost of defense attorney's fees alone—not settlement, not judgment, just the cost of having a lawyer defend you—runs between $150,000 and $200,000 for a case that goes through trial. Cases that settle before trial still routinely cost $50,000 to $100,000 in legal fees. In major metropolitan areas, in complex commercial litigation, or in employment cases, those numbers are significantly higher. A case with multiple parties, extensive discovery, and expert witnesses can easily run into the hundreds of thousands in defense costs alone.

I'm not telling you this to scare you, although it is scary for most people. I'm telling you to put this step in context. Because if there is an insurance policy that covers any of your defense, settlement, or judgment, the financial calculus of this lawsuit changes completely.

What Do I Do Right Now?

Dig out every insurance policy you have. All of them. Business policies, personal policies, umbrella policies, homeowners, professional liability, directors and officers coverage, errors and omissions, commercial general liability, past and current—everything. If you are not sure where your policies are, call your broker and ask them to pull a complete list of every policy they have placed for you.

Actually, do that last part even if you think you have everything, just in case.

Now here's the important part: Do not object to yourself by deciding to not tender to insurance because you think there will be no coverage. Unless it is blatantly not applicable (e.g. a personal car insurance policy on a wrongful termination case), do not deny coverage for yourself by not sending it. Do not look at the summary of the policy, or the declarations page, or even the entire ten thousand page contract, and decide on your own that it probably does not cover this type of claim. You are not an insurance coverage lawyer. Whether a policy covers a claim is frequently not obvious, even to experienced attorneys. Tender to everything and let the professionals sort it out.

Here are some coverage sources that defendants routinely overlook:

- **Homeowners' or Renters' insurance**. If you are being sued personally, your homeowners' policy may provide a defense. This surprises most people. Homeowners policies often contain personal liability coverage that extends to certain civil claims.

- **Umbrella policies**. Personal and commercial umbrella policies sit above your primary coverage and can provide significant additional limits. They also sometimes cover gaps that primary policies exclude. Do not forget them.

- **Directors and Officers insurance**. If you are an officer or director of any company, nonprofit, or board, there may be D&O coverage available. This is frequently forgotten, particularly by small business owners who do not think of themselves as having D&O exposure.

- **Professional liability and Errors and Omissions policies**. If the lawsuit arises from your professional conduct or your business's services, these policies may apply even if the complaint does not use the specific language your policy uses.

- **Automobile policies**. Sometimes coverage applies even if you are not the driver, or you are driving someone else's vehicle.

- **Worker's Compensation policies**. If an employee (and that can include business owners) claims any kind of injury, worker's compensation may be the sole remedy. This is potentially broader than you think.

- **Prior year policies**. Some claims are covered under the policy that was in effect when the alleged conduct occurred, not the policy in effect when the lawsuit was filed. If you have had coverage with different carriers over the years, prior year policies may be relevant.

Tender the Lawsuit

Regardless of whether you used a broker to buy your policies or purchased directly, you should immediately tender the lawsuit to your insurance companies. Look at your policy to determine how to tender the claim. This information should be upfront, and tendering can usually be done by email with a copy of the complaint, demand letter, or petition. Make sure you keep evidence of this tender by email or screenshot. This is better than tendering by telephone because you want irrefutable proof of the tender and the date you did it.

Once the lawsuit is sent, the insurance company is on notice, and the process starts. That's the key step. If the insurance company requests more information before deciding coverage (and this is becoming increasingly common), I suggest you get your lawyer involved. Lawyers experienced in insurance matters will frame your case for coverage better than you can do alone.

Send the Lawsuit to Your Broker, Too

This part is very important, so read it carefully and follow the steps.

Once you have identified your policies, if you used an insurance broker, send a copy of the lawsuit to your broker with explicit written instructions to ***tender for coverage under any and all available policies***. Do this in writing. Do it even though you've already tendered the lawsuit to your insurance company. Keep a copy of this request.

Here is something most people do not know about their broker: your insurance broker has a fiduciary duty to you. Part of that duty includes tendering claims and finding potentially applicable policies on your behalf. The broker doesn't have to ensure you get coverage, but they have to do the ministerial act of tendering and finding policies. If your broker fails to locate an available policy and tender your claim, and then you suffer a loss that policy would have covered, your broker's own professional liability insurance may be on the hook for your defense and liability losses.

Your broker knows this. It's on the licensing exam. When you send written instructions to tender to any and all available policies, you are activating their professional obligation in a way they cannot ignore.

Do not just call and mention the lawsuit in passing. Send it in writing. Say explicitly: *I have been served with the attached lawsuit. Please tender this claim for defense and indemnity coverage to any and all applicable policies you have placed on my behalf.*

What If The Insurance Company Tells Me There Is No Coverage?

There may not be coverage, but you don't have to accept that answer without pushing back. And certainly do not accept it before your lawyer has weighed in.

Insurance companies are not neutral parties in coverage determinations. They have a financial interest in denying coverage, and their adjusters are trained to find reasons to do exactly that. A denial from an adjuster is not a final legal determination. It is the insurance company's opening position.

Coverage questions are sometimes close calls. Policy language changes from year to year. Terms that seem clear are sometimes ambiguous in application. Courts can find coverage where insurers initially denied it, particularly when policy language is susceptible to more than one reasonable interpretation. Under those circumstances, ambiguity is generally construed against the insurer.

There is also the matter of bad faith. Insurance companies that wrongfully deny coverage face significant exposure for bad faith claims in most jurisdictions. The damages for bad faith can exceed the original policy limits. Insurers know this, and a coverage denial that looks firm when you are unrepresented can soften when a lawyer sends a demand letter citing bad faith exposure.

I have negotiated coverage for clients dozens of times after an initial denial. I have walked into cases where other lawyers had already been told there was no coverage—by the other lawyers, by the brokers, and by the adjusters—and found it anyway. In one complex business dispute where all the partners were suing each other, I forced the broker to tender under threat of a malpractice claim, and obtained coverage not just for my client but for several of the other parties whose own lawyers had not bothered to ask.

Tender the claim. If you are denied, tell your lawyer. It could literally save your bacon.

But Won't My Premiums Go Up?

This is the question I get most often at this step, and the answer is: if there's no coverage, then usually not. If there is, your premium may go up, but probably not as much as you think. And it does not matter as much as you think. Personal automobile insurance premiums are the most sensitive to claims, but other policies are usually not as sensitive. For personal policies like homeowner's insurance that do not involve annual audits, a denied claim rarely affects your premium at all.

Business insurers expect businesses to get sued sometimes and consider that in pricing. And here is another reality of business insurance: Every year, when your policies come up for renewal, you go through an underwriting process that includes disclosure of pending claims and litigation. If you are covered by the policy, they will do a "loss-run" to determine the cost of keeping you as a customer, and that is usually how premium increases are determined. You can also find other insurance companies that will be competitive because they don't have a loss-run associated with your business.

When you disclose pending litigation to an underwriter, it will be under penalty of perjury. If you don't disclose lawsuits and get caught, your coverage can be canceled entirely for misrepresentation. So trying to hide the lawsuit to avoid a premium hike is also a poor strategy for that reason.

Because even if your premium goes up, so what? Insurance coverage on a lawsuit is worth multiples of any premium increase you might experience. A paid claim may cause an increase. But compare that to the alternative: paying $150,000 in defense fees and settlement out of your own pocket. There is no version of that math where skipping the tender makes financial sense.

The entire purpose of insurance is to transfer catastrophic financial risk to someone equipped to absorb it. A lawsuit is exactly that kind of risk. Use your insurance.

A Note on Timing

Insurance policies frequently contain notice requirements—provisions that require you to give timely notice of a claim as a condition of coverage. What constitutes "timely" varies by policy and jurisdiction, but the general principle is that earlier is always better. A late tender can give the insurer grounds to deny coverage on procedural grounds entirely separate from the merits of the claim.

Do not sit on this. The same day you calculate your answer deadline and suspend your document destruction is the day you send the lawsuit to your insurance companies and brokers. This is a thirty-minute task with potentially six-figure consequences.

STEP 4 EXECUTIVE SUMMARY

- Pull every insurance policy you have: business, personal, umbrella, homeowners, professional liability, D&O, E&O, automobile, worker's compensation, etcetera, and any prior year policies that were in effect when the alleged conduct occurred.

- Do not object to yourself. Tender to all your insurance companies and let the professionals determine coverage.

- Send a copy of the lawsuit to your broker in writing with explicit instructions to tender for defense and indemnity coverage under any and all available policies. Keep a copy of that communication.

- If you are told there is no coverage, do not accept that as final. Tell your lawyer and have them push back. Coverage denials are sometimes negotiable.

- Do not let premium concerns stop you from tendering. You are required to disclose the lawsuit at renewal anyway. Get the coverage benefit you are already paying for.

- Do this the same day you complete Steps 2 and 3. Notice deadlines in your policies make timing critical.

STEP 5

MAKE A TIMELINE OF EVENTS.

You know what happened. Or at least, you think you do. Right now, sitting with the lawsuit in front of you, the events feel vivid and immediate. You remember the meeting, the email, the conversation, the decision, the accident. You remember who said what and when.

You're also anxious, and you want to get it all out of your head.

Good, take advantage of that energy. (But not by calling your mom.)

Six months from now, under the pressure of litigation, with depositions scheduled and opposing counsel asking pointed questions, you will be surprised how much of that clarity has eroded. Memory is not a recording. It is a reconstruction. Memories degrade quickly under stress, time, and the repeated retelling that litigation demands. The time to capture what you know is right now, while it is fresh, before the lawsuit itself starts to reshape your recollection of the events that gave rise to it.

Write it down today.

A Timeline Saves A Case From Beyond the Grave

It doesn't happen often, but I have had a key witness or a client die during litigation. Cases don't always die with the litigant, however. I had a case once where I worked closely with the client in a lawsuit against his company. I had him prepare a timeline for me, along with notes about documents and witnesses. He was the owner of the company, and this information were things that only he knew.

Sadly, halfway through the case, he suddenly became ill and passed away. After his passing, his business continued through his wife and children. But they knew nothing about the facts of the lawsuit. Because I had the timeline, I was able to complete discovery and find secondary sources (documents mainly) to educate his wife, who was able to testify on behalf of the company.

Lost evidence can really hinder a defense. If we hadn't created that roadmap of information via timeline, we might've lost the case.

What Do I Actually Do?

Start your timeline (whether typed or handwritten) with the following label: ATTORNEY-CLIENT PRIVILEGE AND ATTORNEY WORK PRODUCT.

You are writing this timeline to give to your attorney, as a communication and to help them prepare your defense. Keep it confidential and do not share it with anyone who isn't your attorney. That helps this specific set of notes from becoming discoverable.

1. Write down everything you can remember about the

events that led to this lawsuit.

Organize them in chronological order if you can. Be as complete and honest as you can. Do not make judgments about relevance. Do not edit yourself. Do not write what you wish had happened, or what you think sounds better. Write what actually happened, including the parts that worry you.

This is not a public document. It is not going to the opposing party. It is a communication to your lawyer, and its entire purpose is to give your lawyer the full picture so they can do their job effectively. An incomplete or sanitized timeline is worse than useless. It leaves your lawyer unprepared for the facts that the other side will absolutely find and use.

2. Add questions for your lawyer as you go.

This helps confirm the document is privileged because it is being prepared for your lawyer and isn't a mere recitation of facts. It also records specific questions you have about the facts for your lawyer while they're fresh. Please do not skip this step.

3. Be specific.

Include dates wherever you can remember them, or approximate dates if that is the best you can do. Include names: who was present, who said what, who sent which email. Note where documents exist that support your recollection: contracts, emails, text messages, invoices, photographs. If there are facts that hurt you, write them down. Your lawyer needs to know about the bad facts before opposing counsel surfaces them in discovery or at deposition, not after.

4. Format does not matter.

A bulleted list organized by date is fine. A narrative paragraph by paragraph is fine. Write in columns with annotations if you want.

Use footnotes or interlineations or commenting functions. Use a spreadsheet. Buy a line-ruled composition book as though you're in middle school. Draw flowcharts or diagrams. *Format doesn't matter.* Do whatever allows you to get the information out of your head and onto paper in a way that is clear and organized enough for your lawyer to follow.

A Critical Note on Discoverability

In Steps 1 and 2, I told you that things you write down in connection with this lawsuit are potentially discoverable. That remains true here, and I want to address it directly rather than let it stop you from doing something that is genuinely valuable.

Yes, your timeline is a document. Yes, documents can be subpoenaed. Notes you write to yourself, journals, personal records—all of those are fair game in discovery unless they are protected by a privilege, and they will be requested by the other attorney early on.

You want to maximize the Attorney-Client privilege available to your timeline. That is why you want to label it as privileged. This labeling matters. Notes that you prepare for the express purpose of communicating with your lawyer, or that your lawyer requests you prepare in connection with the lawsuit, carry the strongest available protection from disclosure.

Attorney-client privilege protects confidential communications between you and your lawyer. The Work Product privilege protects materials your lawyer has prepared for litigation—whether they prepare it themselves or have another person (like an expert, a paralegal, or you) prepare it. Your timeline, prepared for the express purpose of sharing with counsel, can qualify for both.

Integrating questions for your lawyer also strengthens the privilege and is an effective strategy for ensuring confidentiality. Many courts hold that "just the facts" is not privileged communication to your lawyer. Facts are discoverable. But facts that are integrated with questions, impressions, and ideas for your lawyer are squarely privileged.

Nothing can guarantee protection from disclosure. A court can still order disclosure if the opposing party makes a sufficient showing that the document was not prepared for your attorney. This is rare, however.

More frequently, the privilege can be waived if you share the document with anyone outside the attorney-client relationship. Which is also why you *must* keep the document confidential and not show it to anyone who isn't your lawyer.

The bottom line: the risk of discoverable timeline notes is real but manageable. The risk of going into litigation without having captured your recollection while it was fresh is worse. Do it. Label it correctly. Share it only with your lawyer.

> **POINTER**: Do not type your timeline into an AI tool, post it to a shared cloud document, email it to friends or family for their input, use it as an *Am I the AH?* post on Reddit, or share it on any platform that isn't strictly confidential communication with counsel. As covered in Step 1, anything you share outside the attorney-client relationship loses its privilege protection and becomes fair game for the other

side. That includes, especially, social media and AI.

Why Your Lawyer Needs A Timeline

Your lawyer is going to ask you for the facts. That conversation is going to happen whether you walk into the office with a timeline or without one. The difference is efficiency, thoroughness, and cost.

A client who arrives at the first consultation with a well-organized timeline of events gives their lawyer a significant head start. The lawyer can read it in advance, identify the key issues, spot the potential problems, formulate a rough litigation plan and budget, and arrive at the consultation with informed, targeted questions rather than spending the first hour reconstructing basic chronology. That saves time. Time is money. *Your* money.

More importantly, a written timeline captures details that oral recollection misses. When you tell the story out loud, you tell it the way you have already told it, shaped by repetition, by what feels important, by what you remember most vividly. When you write it down systematically, working through the timeline date by date, you often surface details you had not thought to mention: a phone call you forgot about, a document you did not immediately realize was relevant, a witness who was present at a critical moment. Those details can change the shape of a defense.

A timeline also helps your lawyer remember the facts of your case as the litigation drags on. Most lawyers have dozens of cases at any given time. And cases can take months to years. What you told them at the first consultation is going to erode from their memory. The timeline helps them remember without filters, repetition, errors, or extra billable hours.

Your Lawyer Needs the Whole Truth, Including the Bad Parts

You should never lie to your doctor, your priest, or your lawyer—even by omission. Your timeline needs to include the facts that reflect badly on you or scare you about your case.

I understand the impulse to leave those out. You are writing a document that feels like it is building your case, and instinct says to put the best version of events on paper. There are also normal emotional reasons you might avoid admitting certain facts, from fear to shame. Resist censoring the facts.

Here is why. The facts are the facts. The plaintiff knows them—or will know them once discovery gets underway. The other side is going to surface every unflattering email, every problematic decision, every moment where your conduct was less than ideal. The question is not whether those facts will come out. They will. The question is whether your lawyer knew about them in advance and had time to prepare for them, or whether they surfaced for the first time at a deposition with opposing counsel capturing your expression on video and your lawyer blindsided.

A lawyer who is blindsided by bad facts at deposition cannot protect you from them. A lawyer who knows about them in advance can contextualize them, anticipate how they will be used, prepare you to address them without making things worse, and sometimes develop arguments that neutralize them entirely.

There is another dimension to this that most clients do not anticipate. Certain statements you make can inadvertently put otherwise protected information "in issue." For example, in most cases, you would be protected from having to disclose your financial records, medical history, or tax returns. But a single poorly chosen statement about your financial condition or your health can waive that protection and open the door to discovery you cannot close again. Your lawyer can only protect you from that trap if they know the full picture. Give it to them.

Full disclosure to your lawyer is not a risk. It is a protection. Your lawyer cannot use information against you—they are bound by confidentiality and professional ethics—but opposing counsel will use every gap in your lawyer's knowledge against you at the worst possible moment. *Even if you feel embarrassed, I promise your lawyer has probably heard worse, and isn't here to judge you.*

Identifying Documents and Witnesses

As you write your timeline, you will naturally begin to remember documents and people connected to the events. Note them as you go.

<u>For documents</u>: Note what the document is, approximately when it was created, who created it, and where it is or was last located. Even if you are not sure whether a document still exists, note it. Your lawyer will want to know about it.

<u>For witnesses</u>: Note anyone who was present at key events, anyone who has relevant knowledge, and anyone you communicated with about the dispute. Include people whose testimony might help you and people whose testimony might not. Your lawyer

needs both lists.

NEVER CONTACT WITNESSES YOURSELF. As discussed in Step 1, that creates risks of witness contamination and, in some circumstances, can raise accusations of improper contact. Let your lawyer manage witness communications.

STEP 5 EXECUTIVE SUMMARY

- Write a complete, honest, chronological timeline of the events that led to this lawsuit while your memory is fresh.
- Include dates, names, documents, and witnesses.
- Label the document: *Attorney-Client Privilege and Attorney Work Product*
- Intersperse questions for your lawyer as you go
- Share it only with your lawyer. Do not email it to friends, type it into an AI tool, or post it anywhere it can be seen by anyone who isn't your lawyer.
- Include the bad facts, and don't fear embarrassment or your attorney using anything against you. Your lawyer is here to protect you, but they cannot protect you from what they do not know.
- Do not contact potential witnesses yourself.

STEP 6

EDUCATE YOURSELF ON THE BASIC LAWSUIT PROCESS.

The lawsuit on your desk feels like a crisis. And in some ways, it is. But it is a slow-moving crisis with a defined sequence of events that unfolds over months or years according to rules that have been developed over centuries.

Understanding that structure will not make the lawsuit disappear, but it will do something almost as valuable: it will replace the formless dread of not knowing what is coming with a clear-eyed picture of what you are actually facing.

Fear of the unknown is almost always worse than the thing itself. This chapter is about what you are facing so that you don't have to proceed in fear.

How Lawyers Defend You Is How They Defend Themselves

Many years ago, a potential client walked into my office and consulted with me about how to defend a lawsuit brought against their business and them personally. After I explained the steps, the potential client asked me: “Pretend you are defending this lawsuit for yourself. How would you handle things differently to make it go away immediately?”

The answer I gave was that my defense wouldn’t change. Lawsuits follow a process. I wouldn’t be able to bring a case to resolution faster for myself than for a client. That’s not how any of this works.

Actually, a slightly more complete answer is that I would do things that are more litigious than what I do for my clients. The reason is that I don’t cost myself billable hours. So I can litigate more aggressively without fear of overrunning a budget. But inflating a client’s bill with speculative litigation is not responsible advocacy, and I have to consider the cost of what I do when I’m charging by the hour. Also, me at scorched earth doesn’t hasten resolution.

The Philosophy Behind Every Lawsuit: Due Process

Before we walk through the mechanics, you need to understand the principle that drives all of it: *due process*.

Due Process isn’t just a phrase in the U.S. Constitution. Due process is required at every step and controls all court procedures. Due Process means both sides get a full and fair opportunity to present their case through a structured series of procedures.

Hard truth: It does not matter whether the lawsuit seems frivolous, vindictive, or built on outright lies. The legal system is not designed to *just take your word for it*—or the plaintiff's, for that matter. It is designed to give both sides the tools to surface evidence, challenge each other's claims, and submit the dispute to a neutral decision-maker.

(At least that's the idea. It's not always perfect in practice.)

Due process is why you cannot simply walk into court and say what every defendant wants to say: "Judge, this is nonsense. The plaintiff is lying. They're trying to extort me! Throw the case out."

All those things may be true. But the judge does not know you. The judge does not know the plaintiff. The judge has no basis for deciding who is telling the truth based on a speech from either side. That is the jury's job, actually, and the jury does not get involved until both sides have had the full opportunity to investigate, gather evidence, and present their case.

Due process is the reason lawsuits take as long as they do. It is also the reason the system works as well as it does. It might not feel that way when you're in the middle of it. But if you've ever experienced truncated procedures—like traffic court, administrative hearings, or small claims—or you've ever been a plaintiff, then you may have some appreciation for the full rules that protect you in general civil litigation.

The Life of a Lawsuit

Every civil lawsuit moves through the same general sequence of phases, though the timeline and complexity vary enormously depending on the court, the type of case, and the parties involved. Here is what you can expect.

Pleadings. If you've just been sued, this is where you are now.

The plaintiff has filed a complaint setting out their claims. You will file a response, such as an answer, a motion to dismiss, or other objection. The pleadings phase establishes what the dispute is officially about and what defenses you are asserting. Motions to dismiss, if filed, can sometimes end the case or narrow it significantly before discovery begins. This phase typically takes one to four months, but it can go longer in complex cases.

Discovery. This is the longest and most expensive phase of litigation, and the one that surprises defendants the most. Discovery is the formal process by which both sides investigate the facts—exchanging documents, answering written questions under oath, and taking depositions. Depositions are sworn testimony given outside of court, recorded by a court reporter, and usable at trial. During discovery, both sides have broad rights to demand information from each other and from third parties.

Discovery is where your evidence preservation from Step 2 pays off, or where failures to preserve come back to haunt you. It is also where the bulk of your legal fees accumulate. Your lawyer will spend hundreds of hours reviewing documents, drafting discovery requests, responding to the other side's demands, and preparing you and your witnesses for depositions. There will almost certainly be disputes about what each side may see, and those disputes will generate their own motions and hearings. Discovery in a moderately complex case can easily take a year or more.

Pretrial Motions. Once discovery closes, both sides typically file motions asking the court to resolve certain issues before trial. The most significant of these is the motion for summary judgment, in which a party argues that the undisputed facts entitle them to win as a matter of law without going to a jury. Summary judgment motions can end cases or dramatically narrow the issues that go to trial. This phase also includes motions about what evidence will be allowed at trial and how the jury will be instructed.

Settlement. Settlement can happen at any point in the litigation—before the answer is filed, during discovery, after summary judgment, or on the courthouse steps the morning of trial. Most cases settle. The pressure to resolve intensifies as the trial date approaches and both sides have a clearer picture of the evidence and their relative risks. Courts frequently require the parties to attempt mediation—a structured negotiation facilitated by a neutral third party—before allowing a case to proceed to trial. I discuss early settlement strategy in more detail in Step 9.

Trial. If the case does not settle, it goes to trial. A jury trial involves jury selection, opening statements, presentation of evidence, witness examination and cross-examination, closing arguments, jury instructions, and verdict. Bench trials and arbitration—trials decided by a judge or arbitrator without a jury—follow a similar structure without the jury components. Trial is the most intense and expensive phase of litigation, and it is where the quality of your trial lawyer matters most, because very few lawyers have appreciable trial experience.

Post-Trial. Even after a verdict, the losing party may file motions challenging the result or pursue an appeal. Appeals can add years to a case. A verdict is not always the end.

How Long Will This Take?

Unless you have a bucket of money you want to hand the plaintiff to "buy the peace" immediately, plan for one to three years from service to resolution, with complex cases sometimes running longer. That timeline feels enormous when you are standing at the beginning of it, and you just want the pain to be over.

I understand the emotional urge to get it over with. I feel that way in conflicts where I'm a party too. Sometimes "it's going to take years of uncertainty" feels intolerable.

That's where understanding the process helps. You can calm your stress and plan around the lawsuit so that you can continue to live your life and operate your business. After a while, you won't think about it except when your lawyer pops up to tell you something new.

To understand why this takes so long, it's helpful to have some perspective on what is going on in the courts. Courts have their own schedules and backlogs. Each judge likely has a thousand cases assigned to their chambers (this is not an exaggeration). Lawyers can have dozens of cases, too. For legal professionals, everything feels like a mad dash all the time. Judges set deadlines that lawyers then negotiate extensions on because they require food and sleep. Or the client needs time to pay the bill. Discovery disputes cause extra delays. Summary judgment briefing takes months. Trial dates get continued. The pace of litigation is almost never what either party wants it to be.

This is one of the reasons I tell business clients to think of litigation as a cost of doing business rather than an acute emergency. An acute emergency demands immediate resolution. Litigation demands sustained, strategic engagement over a long period. Those require different mindsets and different resources.

What It Is Going to Cost

You already have a sense of the defense costs from Step 4. But I want to give you a fuller picture here, because unrealistic expectations about cost are one of the most common sources of conflict between clients and their lawyers.

First of all, the below costs are for regular civil lawsuits. Small claims, administrative claims, arbitration, and class actions all have their own economics.

Second, the fees noted in Step 4—$50,000 to $200,000—represent the cost of your defense lawyer alone. They do not include expert witness fees, which can run $10,000 to $50,000 or more per expert (although experts are not always required in cases). They also do not include court costs, filing fees, deposition transcripts, or the cost of document review platforms in complex cases. They do not include the cost of your own time or the cost to your business or job or peace of mind caused by disruption. And they do not include any settlement amount or judgment.

None of this is meant to demoralize you. It is meant to give you an accurate picture so you can make informed decisions throughout the process, including specifically on how aggressively to fight, when to consider settlement, and how to budget for what is coming.

A Few Things Worth Knowing

These are responses to common misconceptions or questions that I hear regularly.

1. Most lawsuits are not frivolous. The plaintiff had to find a lawyer, pay a filing fee, and commit to a process that is costly and unpleasant for them too. That does not mean the claims are all meritorious, but it means they believed they had a case to pursue with enough conviction to invest in it. And then they convinced a lawyer, too. Take it seriously.

2. Prepare for trial, but expect to settle. Statistically, only about ten percent of lawsuits go to trial, and only about ten percent of those reach a verdict. If you are the one in a hundred whose case goes to verdict, you have roughly even odds of winning, although every case turns on its own facts. The overwhelming probability is that your case will settle at some point. That does not mean you prepare as if it will. You prepare for trial and let settlement happen when the conditions are right. A plaintiff's lawyer who knows your defense attorney has never seen the inside of a courtroom is a plaintiff's lawyer with more leverage. A plaintiff's lawyer who knows your attorney has tried and won cases like this one is a plaintiff's lawyer who is more motivated to settle on reasonable terms.

3. Discovery will be the hard part. Most of the cost, most of the time, and most of the stress of litigation happens during discovery. This is where you will be asked to produce thousands of documents, sit for a deposition and answer questions under oath for hours, and watch your lawyer fight with opposing counsel over minutiae that may or may not matter in the end.

4. Nuisance value is real. Some plaintiffs, and more importantly their attorneys, understand that the cost of defending a lawsuit can exceed the cost of settling it, regardless of the merits. They file cases knowing that a defendant will pay to make them go away. This is called nuisance-value litigation, and it exists. Your lawyer will help you assess whether you are facing it and how to respond strategically.

Why This Knowledge Matters Right Now

You need to understand the structure of a lawsuit before you hire a lawyer, because this knowledge will help you ask the right questions during the hiring process. What is this lawyer's approach to the pleadings phase? How does she handle discovery disputes? Has she tried cases like this one? How has she gotten cases like this one to settlement, and at what stage? What does she think the key issues in your case will be?

A little knowledge transforms you from a passive recipient of legal services into an informed participant in your own defense. That participation—asking the right questions, understanding what your lawyer is doing and why, being prepared for each phase rather than surprised by it—is one of the most valuable things you can bring to your own case.

You are in this now. Understanding what "this" means is the first step to navigating it well.

STEP 6 EXECUTIVE SUMMARY

- Lawsuits move through defined phases: pleadings, discovery, pretrial motions, settlement attempts, trial, and post-trial. Understand each one.

- Due process means both sides get a full and fair hearing.

The court will not just take your word for it, no matter how stupid you think the case is. Plan for the full process.

- Expect one to three years from service to resolution. Budget accordingly, both financially and emotionally.
- Most cases settle. Prepare for trial anyway. At the very least, your negotiating leverage depends on it.
- Discovery is the longest, most expensive, and most stressful phase. Evidence preserved in Step 2 will help.
- Use this knowledge to ask better questions when interviewing lawyers. A lawyer who can explain their strategy for each phase is a lawyer who will usually be one step ahead of the other side.
- You're in this whether you like it or not. Understanding the process is how you stop being nervous and start managing it.

STEP 7, PART I

HOW TO HIRE THE BEST LAWYER FOR YOU.

Over the years, I have developed a reputation for taking difficult, messed-up legal problems and fixing them for my clients. I am not sure how I ended up in this niche. But I can tell you that nearly every terrible legal mess that has been dropped on my lap has one thing in common: the client did not hire a lawyer—or a good lawyer—or listened to their lawyer—until it was nearly too late.

Not investing in adequate counsel from the outset typically resulted in far more stress and expense than if I'd been hired before the problems compounded. Using lawyers proactively more would save Americans (and especially small businesses) millions in legal fees every month.

But the biggest challenge that I've seen to this is money. Lawyers are expensive, and people don't want to spend it. *Ever*. People genuinely hate lawyers, and legal fees irritate them. They don't see the value, assume that lawyers are trying to cheat them, or they are angry that they are being sued and think that *it's just not fair* that they should have to absorb defense costs when they did nothing wrong. Business owners can also be blind to the risks they're flirting with when they run their companies without regular legal counsel, and may even get away with it for years before disaster strikes.

But not you. You have read six chapters of this book. You have seen what happens when defendants destroy evidence, miss deadlines, ignore insurance, and walk into depositions unprepared. By now you understand that this is not a problem you can manage alone. The question is not whether to hire a lawyer. The question is how to hire the *right* lawyer.

> **POINTER**: If you are a registered business (whether a corporation or an LLC), you cannot represent the business in court unless you are a licensed attorney. You can represent yourself (but not others), but because of the stakes and complexity of the process, it is not recommended.

What Happened When I Hired The Wrong Lawyer

Despite my years of experience and training, and being a generally responsible person, I have made just about every mistake a person and a business owner can make. I've never judged anyone who came to me with a messed-up situation because, honestly, *girl, same.*

Many years ago, I brought my employment law practice to a well-respected firm as a partner. I shut down my firm, wound down the business (which is not a quick or easy process), and transferred my cases to the new firm. A month later, I received a cancer diagnosis.

The firm was displeased that I needed to take leave to tend to my health. I was, however, terribly sick and immediately traumatized by the situation. My recovery from my first round of treatment was slow, and while I was still on leave, the firm fired me.

Long story short, I was devastated financially and emotionally by this. I have complex PTSD already, and this experience did that condition absolutely no favors. At the time, the statute of limitations for wrongful termination and disability discrimination was one year. I was not capable of handling this on my own—too upsetting—and so I sought legal representation.

I ran into a problem, however. The firm was well-networked in my city, and no one wanted to go against them. Actually, at one point, they told me to, "Do the right thing for your career," and not sue them.

I'm not that meek, even when sick. So I used my own law firm employees (I had restarted my business by then) to sue and eventually convinced a law school friend to take my case.

Unfortunately, my friend was not the right lawyer for this case. We ended up in a paperwork hole, and I had to handle my own case in an emergency, which I was not emotionally equipped to do. After damage was done to the case, I had to let him go. I called half the lawyers in town and eventually found someone else. My next lawyer did a good job rescuing the case. We settled it for a nice sum, but for somewhat less than I think I would've managed had the case been handled correctly from the start.

So, yes, I hired the wrong lawyer for my own case *in my own area of expertise*. So I can tell you, when your emotions, your health, your business, your finances, your *life* are on the line, it makes a difference.

Reasons People Give Me For Why They Try to DIY Legal Work

Here's what I learned being on the client side of the attorney-client relationship (more than just that one time, by the way—I *am* a business owner). To make a good decision, you need to know your own feelings about lawyers and identify any resistance you have to hiring one. Until you know what your sticking points are, you will not be able to find a lawyer who can truly meet your needs. Think about whether you can commit to hiring a lawyer whom you can trust on a deep level. Because that is genuinely required.

If you have before, or you are now considering skipping the lawyer to do things yourself, you aren't alone. Do any of these reasons for such a decision sound familiar?

- "I am a sophisticated and successful person. I understand things."
- "I can read about this legal issue on the internet or using AI."
- "I don't like lawyers."
- "I can call the plaintiff and reason with them."
- "I don't think this is a big deal."
- "I haven't been contacted by the plaintiff since being sued. No news is good news."

•"Lawyers are too expensive and a rip-off."

•"This issue is frivolous."

•"Why should I have to do anything? I didn't do anything wrong."

If you are hesitant to hire a lawyer, I bet that you have made one or more of those statements, even if just to yourself.

I challenge you to consider this statement thoughtfully: those reasons are nothing more than rationalizations of deeper feelings (usually pride, fear, or shame). Or money is tight (as it is for so many these days) and you would really just *rather not*.

This is not an insult. These rationalizations are understandable responses to a legal situation.

From the outside looking in, legal work may seem like a bunch of needless paperwork causing lots of delays. Can't you just write what you want in the contract without a bunch of hassle? Maybe lawyers seem like they are creating work just to charge you when everyone is otherwise happy without the fuss.

If you are dealing with a conflict, maybe the legal problem seems unfair or overblown. It surprises even sophisticated people that legal conflicts are not easily resolved with discussion and reasoning, or by just telling the judge your side of the story.

Or the legal situation causes you anxiety. And you would rather not pay attention to it, much less spend money on a lawyer. (I really get this one. As someone who experiences avoidance behavior as a symptom of my PTSD, I could easily stick a problem in a drawer and ignore it, if I didn't actively force myself to make better decisions.) Legal fees will cause you further stress by reminding you of the problem. And that goes double if legal fees are a strain for you financially.

Maybe you do not want to admit that you have anxiety or fear. Few people do. And you don't have to admit it to me. Admitting it to yourself is all you need to do.

To avoid legal disaster, you must recognize these rationalizations for what they are. Then you can overcome them and make healthier choices.

Know What You Don't Know

You're a smart, capable person. I respect your intelligence and your ability to problem-solve. You've survived Earth this long, after all.

But law is not intuitive. A truly wise man recognizes that which he does not know. A wise business owner delegates tasks to experts who are better than she at those tasks instead of trying to do it all and be everything. There is no shame in asking for help from an expert.

Lawyers are experts. Consider that a lawyer goes through three years of law school, passes a bar exam, and then spends years practicing and learning from other lawyers until they are competent enough to manage complex cases directly for clients.

The lawmakers (legislators and judges) are all lawyers and speak the language of law. As a consequence of lifelong training, they apply principles of law that are taught and not necessarily "commonsense." Legal language is second nature to lawyers, but is frequently lost on non-lawyers.

Perhaps you dislike that the law is not easily decipherable by the regular person, but that is the reality. It is also not a matter of simply looking up information on the Internet or using an AI chatbot. Law is not the rote application of written rules. (I actually have this argument sometimes with my brother, who has a doctorate in AI—it can't replace the justice system reliably because law is about human behavior, and humans aren't robots.)

Good lawyers can predict potential future problems (especially when it comes to business deals and contract drafting) based on all the weird things they have seen over the years. They can tell you why they write something a certain way. They apply practical risk analysis, weighing factors that may not occur to you. They understand the customs of local courts and judges and have relationships and community resources.

And the best lawyers understand human behavior and can manipulate it (in an ethical, non-evil way). Negotiations, written advocacy, and trials are each art forms requiring a delicate understanding of humans. Even if your chats with an AI bot weren't discoverable, its advice is not reliable because it cannot understand humanity in the same way a human can.

Skillful lawyers do not rely solely on logic or rote memorization of "black letter" law. Nor are they mindless, aggressive bullies. Skillful lawyers are more like martial arts masters who know when to use force, when to stay calm, and when to apply pressure.

Believing that you can understand the complexities of the rules that govern society—which have developed over thousands of years and in response to millions of situations—by reading an article on a website is silly if you think about it. AI is trained by these same sources and does not have the faculty of judgment to apply.

Trying to practice amateur law is as absurd as practicing amateur medicine. And the consequences can be just as devastating. This is not the lawyer's fault. All the rules developed over time because people need help to get along. Lawyers didn't invent human nature. Law is fundamentally about human relationships. Law is the rules we use to govern how we treat each other.

There are bad lawyers, sure. There are greedy lawyers, and there are immoral lawyers. But that is no different from the rest of the population. Sadly, the truth is, sometimes people will cheat you. Sometimes relationships you have with people will break and turn bitter. Sometimes shit happens and everyone looks out for themselves. Sometimes people will betray you.

It is not the lawyer who makes people flawed. The law is the complicated, messy, time-consuming way in which we deal with reality. The lawyer gets you through the mess.

Just like when you have surgery and you have to trust the anesthesiologist and the surgeon to get you through it, trust your lawyer. Make peace with the fact that you cannot do this yourself, and it's going to at times be frightening and expensive. Until you do that, you will struggle with the attorney-client relationship.

STEP 7, PART ONE EXECUTIVE SUMMARY

- Nearly every legal disaster I have cleaned up started with a client who waited too long to hire a lawyer, hired the wrong one, or refused to listen to the one they had. Do not be that client.

- If you are a registered business entity, you cannot represent the company in court unless you are a licensed attorney. You must hire counsel.

- Identify your resistance to hiring a lawyer—pride, fear, shame, cost anxiety, avoidance—and recognize it for what it is. It is not reason. It is rationalization.

- Law is not intuitive, not Googleable, and not something you can outsource to an AI. It is a discipline developed over centuries and applied through judgment that comes only from training and experience.

- Good lawyers predict problems, apply practical risk analysis, understand local courts and judges, and read human behavior well enough to use it strategically. None of that is replicable by a non-lawyer or a chatbot.

- There are bad lawyers, just as there are bad doctors. That is not a reason to go without one. It is a reason to choose carefully.

- Make peace with the fact that you need help, that it will cost money, and that at times it will be frightening. Until you do, you will struggle with the attorney-client relationship and undermine your own defense.

STEP 7, PART 2

HOW TO HIRE THE BEST LAWYER FOR YOU.

So now that you are comfortable with the idea of hiring a lawyer, you need to know how to go about it. Most people turn to the internet at this point. Or they call around to ask for a referral.

There is absolutely nothing wrong with these methods. Online presentations and personal references are a great way to vet lawyers before you waste time talking to them. But that being said, a bunch of stuff that lawyers put online to impress you is just a display of colorful feathers and entirely unimportant.

Don't Hire A Peacock.

I once worked with a lawyer who is the epitome of the peacock. He was bombastic and bragged. He would name-drop. He would encourage the client to be aggressive, and he would showboat when the client was around to prove how "tough" he was and how intimidating he would be to the other lawyers.

The client loved it.

But here's the truth: the opposing lawyers were not intimidated. Lawyers are on the receiving end of threats and bombast all the time. And you don't become a litigation lawyer if you are timid. Never assume your opposing lawyers are shrinking violets, because they're not.

All his showboating did was create more work for all of us and sour relationships between counsel, making the case impossible to settle. This cost the client more money. This lawyer also would have malpracticed if I had not been there quietly executing a sophisticated legal strategy while he strutted around convincing the client how impressive and aggressive he is.

The fact is, most things lawyers use to sell you on their services are unimportant. (Lawyers, like everyone else selling things, use the same nonsense advertising and marketing strategies that other industries use.) So here, in no particular order, is a list of credentials that don't matter, and a few that do.

1. Rankings and awards

A bit of honesty here: When I ran a larger practice, I prominently displayed my 10.0 Avvo rating and my SuperLawyers and AV-Rating badges, along with half a dozen other awards on my website. The truth is, people like them. Other lawyers are impressed. People think it means I'm a good lawyer.

And I *am* a good lawyer. But I'm not a good lawyer because Avvo or SuperLawyers or Martindale says so. Those rating systems, like all rating systems, are flawed. I know people rated as a 10 out of 10 on Avvo who got there after practicing law for only two years. I can categorically say, no matter how smart, no lawyer is a perfect 10 practitioner after a mere two years' experience. But they did all the right things to market themselves on the internet, and that is why they are well-ranked.

Bad lawyers definitely slip through on ratings, too. I know some real hacks that are well-ranked through clever marketing. I also know some great but incompetent guys who are socially popular enough that they do well with peer-review rankings like Martindale. You do not want a guy whose highest talent is that he could be your drinking buddy.

Awards also usually flirt with "pay-to-play." Committees choose the winners of most awards based on factors that they do not share. One may suspect that one factor they consider is the likelihood that a lawyer or their firm will purchase advertising. (I hate to break this to you, but actually nearly all industry awards operate this way.) Awards and rankings are great marketing, but they actually don't tell you anything substantive.

2. Guarantees

It is unethical for a lawyer to guarantee a certain result in your case. We are legally prohibited from doing it. If a lawyer promises you a result or tells you a case is easy, a slam-dunk or without risk ... RUN! This lawyer is just telling you what you want to hear in order to get your business. He plans to figure it out later, or maybe he doesn't care if you are ultimately disappointed.

A common complaint about lawyers is that we equivocate. You want an answer, not just a bunch of possibilities and probabilities. But the best I will ever tell a client is that their position is strong and therefore they have an 80% chance at winning. Too many things can knock the car off the rails for me to say any higher than that. And many times, a client's chances are worse than that. Whenever possible, I present multiple scenarios of varying acceptability that I can aim for.

Life and law are uncertain. And any good, truth-telling lawyer will say the same. A lawyer who appeals solely to your desire for good news is not providing you meaningful advice or professional service.

3. A Harvard degree and a Rolex

Lawyers may use a show of wealth and school pedigrees in order to prove they are skillful and worthy of being hired. These things are not the best indicators of a good lawyer. Lots of bad lawyers went to Harvard, and lots of good lawyers went to the local law school (and vice versa). I know this from personal experience.

One of the most incompetent and unethical lawyers I have ever had the displeasure of meeting wore a Rolex, drove a Bentley, and went to an Ivy league. He fleeced every client who crossed his desk, and now spends a lot of time commenting on Fox News—and using that credential to sell even more of his subpar, over-priced services.

Neither a fancy office nor a degree from Harvard are bad things. But they aren't important things.

4. Big Money Wins

If you have a wrongful death case against Tesla, you want a lawyer with seven-figure verdicts at jury trial under his belt. That guy knows how to sell a big case to a jury against an aggressive company, and that is a particular skill. But most of the time, asking a lawyer how much money he has won is not that useful. It is even less useful when a lawyer claims his firm has recovered millions for his clients (this is not that hard to do in a volume practice or even with just a steady flow of cases settled with mediocre results).

In fact, most lawyers are transactional or administrative lawyers and therefore have no win-loss record. Lots of lawyering work has nothing to do with lawsuits. Criminal defense lawyers plea bargain most things, and conviction rates are 98% of cases that are not pled, so you cannot judge the quality of a criminal defense lawyer by their win-loss ratio.

Similarly, civil defense lawyers may settle most cases and therefore have few outright wins, and even fewer money recoveries (since the aim of defense is the opposite). But they may have achieved consistently excellent results for their clients, given the circumstances. Indeed, only 1% of civil cases go to trial through verdict. And so the vast majority of lawyers have never even stood before a jury.

Of those who have, even the best ones have lost a case. Anyone who says they've never lost a case is either dishonest or has not tried enough cases to have a loss. The best trial lawyers lose sometimes.

You will need to ask yourself first whether you even need a trial lawyer. Because true trial lawyers are rare, they command a premium price. But if you are in a lawsuit of any value, you probably want a trial lawyer on the team. They know how to set up cases early in ways that lawyers without trial experience cannot fully replicate.

Essential Qualifications

There are some basic qualifications any attorney you hire must have. If the lawyer does not meet these specific qualifications, no amount of amazing media appearances or industry accolades will make up for it.

1. Is the Lawyer Licensed in Your Jurisdiction?

In order to represent you, the lawyer must be licensed to practice law in the jurisdiction of your legal issue. Jurisdiction refers to which court has power over you, your lawsuit, your transaction or business, or your property. Usually, jurisdiction is the state you live in, but not always.

If you are suing or dealing in a transaction, then you should start with lawyers in your state. If you are defending a lawsuit, start with lawyers in the same state as the lawsuit you are defending.

Jurisdiction can be complicated, however, so if it is not obvious which state's laws apply. When you interview a lawyer, ask whether he is licensed to practice in the state where jurisdiction lies and whether the jurisdiction could change. This is an elementary issue. Sometimes lawyers don't think about it, which is a sign of sloppiness. If the lawyer doesn't consider jurisdiction first off, then he or she may have poor skills.

2. Practices in Your Area of Law

There is a joke lawyers make about a lawyer who does not specialize: he practices "door law"—as in, anything that walks through the door. Lawyers who practice door law may be incompetent when it comes to your particular issue. You want a lawyer with relevant experience.

When you are first looking to hire a lawyer, try to identify the kind of lawyer you need. For example, if you are dealing with a contract or transaction, then you need a lawyer who handles business and contracts, not a divorce lawyer or a patent lawyer.

If you've been sued, you probably want a lawyer who has trial skills in civil litigation. A criminal lawyer with tons of trial experience is not the right lawyer, despite all the trial experience, because criminal procedures are materially different from civil procedures. In civil law, there are literally a hundred distinct practice areas.

Most civil lawyers practice in several related areas, and you should ask about them.

3. Special Licenses and Court Admissions

This isn't typical, but some lawyers have special licenses that are necessary for your legal needs. The most obvious of these are patent lawyers. No lawyer can file a patent for you unless he is also admitted to practice before the patent office. You have to hire a patent specialist for this work.

Other areas of legal specialization may include admiralty law, bankruptcy law, or admission to special Federal, administrative, and international courts. Some states allow voluntary certified specialization in areas like family law or criminal law. Such voluntary "specializations" aren't required to practice in these areas of law. Rather, they denote someone who has taken an extra test to show a certain level of experience. Most civil law practice areas do not have specializations like this.

How to Interview and Hire A Lawyer

Admittedly, this is the hardest part of the process. I just told you that most of the sales materials lawyers present you are useless. I suggest that what you really need to look for are key interpersonal and intellectual traits that define the hard and soft skills of an effective lawyer.

1. Wisdom

Good judgment, varied life and business experiences, and a results-driven, practical approach means the lawyer has wisdom. Wisdom is what will get you the best results long term, even if it means foregoing instant gratification or hearing the news you want to hear.

2. A student of humanity

The famous Supreme Court Justice Oliver Wendall Holmes said, "The life of the law has not been logic; it has been experience." What this means is that the law is created around the human experience and all the things that make us function together in society.

Without getting too philosophical on you, consider that the law boils down to standards for how we treat one another (whether it is in our criminal codes, our contracts, or our civil rights). Legal applications by judges and juries are therefore as varied as the human experience of each one of those people. The best lawyers understand this.

That is why you need a lawyer who is courageous and mature, who listens, and who is articulate. But most importantly, you need a lawyer who possesses and understands how to use *empathy*.

A lawyer without empathy will never understand you, the other people in your deal or case, or a judge and jury. He will never understand the easiest path to victory or to negotiating and closing a settlement deal. He will not be elegantly persuasive.

Many lawyers read the law and try to apply it to all situations by rote. This "all problems are a nail" approach will not serve you as the client. The "art" in practicing law is what separates the few, best lawyers from the thousands of average lawyers.

3. Intellectual curiosity and hard skills

The best lawyers are always learning. They acquire and practice legal, intellectual, and social skills. They show interest in the law as an intellectual pursuit, and they are aware of and can apply principles from many different legal disciplines.

In civil litigation, you must also evaluate how well a lawyer writes. The main job duty of all civil lawyers, including courtroom trial lawyers, is writing. This is an essential skill. A case can be won or lost on written motions alone. A letter can solve a problem. A tight agreement can prevent future problems.

In the same vein, a lawyer must be detailed. In law, the devil is in the details. A lawyer who is sloppy and unconcerned by the minutiae of law is bad at his job.

There is a saying that, "How you write is how you think." (This is actually a paraphrase of something Oscar Wilde once said.) While this might be an overstatement for any who do not write for a living, it is an excellent rubric for lawyers. A lawyer who can write a blog, article, or brief that explains complex legal ideas simply is a lawyer who can also explain your case to judges and juries simply.

Written work also shows the lawyer's personality, persuasiveness, empathy, and values. It shows how detailed and professional they are. Do they have a lot of typos? Did they use AI to write a bunch of keyword-stuffed, buzzy, or generalized information? Is the information well-organized? Is it clear? Does it evoke emotion? Are you convinced by the end?

You do not have to read everything a lawyer writes. But seeking writing samples is a good way to vet a lawyer.

4. Listens and responds directly

This may be the fastest way you can weed out lawyers who are unsuitable once you start interviewing and consulting with them. Most lawyers are terrible at listening and responding to direct questions. The right lawyer *for you* listens to you and works to achieve the results you desire. The right lawyer *for you* understands you and answers your questions without equivocation. If the lawyer cannot deliver the result you request, she should say so. The best lawyers are courageous and moral enough to tell the truth and to give bad news.

A lawyer should also not jump to conclusions when diagnosing a problem and recommending a litigation plan. Although after a lot of cases, patterns do emerge that lawyers can predict, a lawyer who does not listen to all the facts is bound to miss important information and arrive at the wrong conclusions.

Things to Consider After Interview and Before Hire

As you interview lawyers, evaluate the following intangibles:

•How was the experience in dealing with the law firm's staff?

•Was the lawyer prompt and considerate of your time?

•Did the lawyer listen to you?

•Did the lawyer address your concerns directly?

•Did the lawyer exhibit forthrightness? (Examples may be that the lawyer will tell you that she would need to research a particular legal issue or that she would have to spend some time thinking about a question you posed. Another example of forthrightness is when a lawyer tells you the downsides and risks of your legal problem, as well as the possible upsides.)

•Did the lawyer give you a concrete plan on how to handle your matter?

•Did the lawyer demonstrate skill and mastery over the subject matter?

•Did the lawyer ask questions and appear thoughtful before

giving you advice?

•Is the lawyer articulate?

•Did the lawyer give you her full attention during your meeting?

•Was the lawyer professional?

•Was the lawyer respectful of you and treat you with collegiality and empathy?

•Do you like the lawyer?

•Do you trust the lawyer?

Lawyers are funny people. Many lack basic social skills, can be rude and aggressive, or suffer from arrogance. A quirky lawyer is okay, but jerks make bad trial lawyers. That only works on TV. In real life, judges and juries notice arrogance, inefficiency, inattention, and aggression. Such a lawyer is not persuasive in court.

STEP 7, PART TWO EXECUTIVE SUMMARY

- Most of what lawyers use to market themselves is noise. Learn to filter it.
- Avoid peacocks: lawyers who perform toughness and tell you what you want to hear instead of doing the actual work.
- Rankings and awards are marketing, not professional merit.
- A lawyer who guarantees a result is lying to get your business. Run.
- Law school pedigree, fancy offices, and big money win

claims are not reliable indicators of skill. Judge the work, not the packaging.

- Confirm the lawyer is licensed in the correct jurisdiction and practices in relevant areas of law.
- The traits that actually matter are wisdom, empathy, intellectual curiosity, technical skill, and the ability to listen and respond directly.
- Whenever possible, read the lawyer's writing before you meet them. How they write is how they think.
- In the interview, evaluate whether the lawyer listened, asked good questions, gave you a concrete plan, gave you straight advice, and treated you like a partner rather than a transaction.
- Arrogant, inattentive, and aggressive are not acceptable traits, and they make bad trial lawyers.

STEP 7, PART 3

How to hire the best lawyer for you.

Pricing A Lawyer

Without fail, every prospective client I have asks one question: "What is this going to cost me?"

It's a fair question.

The answer, unfortunately, is rarely a simple one. It usually involves some horribly broad range like, "between $5000 and $150,000 if it goes to trial in two years."

The only way you can be sure of the fee is if it is a flat fee. And, frankly, very few lawyers will offer civil litigation defense on a flat fee, for lots of reasons. The truth is, how attorneys price their services can be an entire book in itself. It's a huge topic that draws strong opinions from within the profession.

But for your purposes today, there are some threshold decisions you need to make about fees.

Price vs. Value

First, you need to decide whether you are going to shop based on price, or based on value. I don't recommend that you shop based on price. It can be penny-wise but pound-foolish. Ideally, you want the best lawyer because your business, property, money, and life are on the line. Why would you go for a discount professional when so much is as stake? You want the best, and the best lawyers are typically not the cheapest lawyers.

There is also a distinction between price and value. A lawyer who offers a lower hourly rate may be cheaper in price, but a worse value. He may not be as efficient, experienced, or capable as a more expensive lawyer. Ultimately, he may deliver you a worse result, or take far longer to get there than the more expensive lawyer, which actually ends up costing you more money than if you had gone with the more expensive lawyer to begin with.

Price should not be your foremost qualification for a lawyer. Value should be.

To make a rational decision about this, consider what is at stake and try to put a value on it.

- How much money is at issue?
- How important is it to you to win versus settle?
- How vulnerable is your business or property, and how much is it worth over your lifetime to build and protect it?
- How much is your time worth in dealing with legal problems or losing ground in your business?

Value is what the lawyer makes you or saves you in addressing your legal problem. That is what matters. Pricing can be a part of value as a larger equation.

If you pay a lawyer $1000 per hour, is he three times more valuable or more efficient than the lawyer at $350 an hour? Will he deliver a superior result that saves you thousands or more? Will he use his lower-priced staff to do routine work but supervise the strategy and handle the specialized work (such as negotiations or trial)? Does the firm offer a holistic approach to your legal matters? What kind of client experience will you have working with them?

That is not to say the most expensive lawyer is always the better lawyer. Some lawyers charge more but do not deliver superior results to the lower-rate lawyer. You need a lawyer who understands your goals and can map out the path to get there. As part of that map, she should be able to give you some indication of the cost along the way.

After you consider the overall value of the services you need rendered, you will have a better idea of how much you should pay for them. If a lawsuit has only $20,000 at stake but the lawyer is going to charge you $300 per hour for 100 hours ($30,000), then you lose $10,000 and that is not a good trade. But if you have $1,000,000 at stake and the lawyer charges you $150,000, then you gain $850,000, and so you have gained significant value, even with a more expensive lawyer.

Alternative Pricing Models

Most lawyers and law firms bill by the hour. That means you will be charged every time your lawyer talks to you (or anyone) about your case, emails you (or anyone) about your case, or even just thinks about your case. (As an aside, you want a lawyer to think about your case so that she delivers a superior result, so you do not want to discourage gray matter activity over bill sensitivity.)

Unfortunately, hourly billing also means that they will bill for the amount of work they do, not the value that work delivers to you. That means your lawyer is actually paid more to be inefficient and is not incentivized to get you good results as fast as possible. Some lawyers will take advantage of this to earn more money. Although the best ones won't, in part because they get plenty of work without milking a matter.

Flat-fee billing is superior to hourly billing in that it shifts the incentive. It encourages your lawyer to be strategic and efficient, or they will end up working a lot of time for less profit. Flat fees also focus on value. Think about it: do you really care if it takes your lawyer ten hours or a thousand hours to get you that million-dollar savings? What you want is the result. That result has a value. And it should be up to the lawyer (as the professional) to figure out how to deliver that value as effectively as possible.

Monthly retainers are essentially flat fees for a block of time. The lawyer does as little or as much work as is required in a month for a set fee, subject to certain parameters. This continues until the legal matter is completed or the lawyer-client relationship is terminated. The lawyer earns the fee by setting aside the time and capacity to do the work for the client, whether it is ultimately needed. Monthly retainers split the difference of risk and incentives between the client and lawyer, and are analogous to having a salaried employee.

In litigation, is unlikely that you'll find a lawyer willing to bill anything other than hourly, though. But seriously consider lawyers who offer alternative billing arrangements if you meet one. It'll make the legal process easier to budget and less painful. And you will be able to make legal decisions based on what is good for the case or your business rather than just choosing less work to keep the bill down.

Hard Costs vs. Legal Fees

As a quirk of legal vocabulary, there is a distinction between legal *fees* and legal *costs*. When a lawyer discusses fees, they are referring to their pay for their time and efforts. That is also the part that is negotiable.

But legal fees are only part of the financial picture. The other part is costs, sometimes called disbursements or out-of-pocket expenses, and they can add up to a significant sum that surprises clients who budgeted only for the hourly rate.

Hard costs are expenses your lawyer incurs on your behalf and passes on to you. They are separate from and in addition to legal fees, and they accrue whether your lawyer bills hourly, flat fee, or on retainer.

Hard costs in civil litigation typically include:

- Court filing fees
- Process server fees
- Court reporter and deposition transcript fees. Every deposition and reported court hearing requires a certified reporter, and transcripts are billed by the page or by the word
- Expert witness fees

- Mediation or arbitration fees, which are usually split between the parties
- Document reproduction and electronic discovery platform costs in document-heavy cases
- Legal research and investigation fees, such as using specialized databases for legal research, or running background searches and skip traces
- Postage, courier, and travel expenses if your lawyer must appear in a distant court

For most of these costs (especially court costs, process server fees, and court reporter fees), the lawyer has little choice but to incur them and cannot negotiate the price for you. They will expect you to reimburse them for advancing these expenses on your behalf.

Ask your lawyer upfront how costs are handled. Some lawyers require a separate cost retainer in addition to a fee retainer. Some invoice costs alongside fees. Some front costs and reconcile at the end. You need to know which arrangement applies to your engagement so that cost invoices do not arrive as a surprise.

> **POINTER**: If your case has mandatory mediation or arbitration provisions, the third-party mediators and arbitrators will typically cost thousands to tens of thousands, and in some classes of cases (consumer, employment), the defendant will bear most or all of these expenses.

POINTER: Expert witness fees deserve special attention because they can be substantial. Experts typically charge $300-$500 per hour or more for their time, including preparation, review of documents, and testimony. A single expert case can easily run $10,000 or more. Discuss this with your lawyer when laying out the litigation plan and budget.

The practical takeaway is this: when you are budgeting for litigation, get an estimate of both components—fees and hard costs—and understand that both are variable. Expert witnesses in particular are a wildcard and very expensive. If your case requires one or more experts, ask your lawyer early what that is likely to cost and factor it into your planning.

STEP 7, PART THREE EXECUTIVE SUMMARY

- Every client wants to know what their case will cost. The honest answer is a range, and that range is wide because litigation is unpredictable.
- Shop on value, not price. A cheaper lawyer who delivers a worse result or takes longer to get there often costs more in the end.
- To assess value, consider what is actually at stake: the money at issue, the impact on your business, and what a

poor result would cost you over time.

- Most lawyers bill by the hour. Hourly billing incentivizes work, not results, but few lawyers will deviate from this model in litigation.

- Flat fees and monthly retainers shift the incentive toward efficiency and strategy. Ask whether either is available for your matter.

- Understand the difference between legal fees—what you pay your lawyer for their work—and hard costs, which are out-of-pocket expenses passed through to you on top of fees.

- Ask your lawyer how costs are handled, billed, and retainered. Do not let cost invoices arrive as a surprise.

STEP 8

ANALYZE YOUR DAMAGES EXPOSURE AND BUILD A DEFENSE BUDGET.

One of the most disorienting things about being served with a lawsuit is the damages demand somewhere in the complaint. Plaintiffs routinely demand staggering sums, and that number lands like a physical blow before you have any context for what it actually means. Is it real? Is it inflated? Could a court actually award that? What are you genuinely exposed to?

I call the damages demand, "the Dr. Evil ransom number."

That is about how seriously I take that number. But that doesn't mean you aren't facing a genuine threat. Understanding what you are actually facing as a financial liability, and what defending the case is going to cost with that risk in mind, is one of the most important conversations you will have with your lawyer, and you will have it much more productively if you walk in with some basic knowledge of how damages work.

How Can You Live With Yourself?

I was hired by a confident businessman years ago on a case that involved a minor mistake under a particular statute. As is sometimes the case with highly successful people who hire me, he did not believe me when I told him what all the damages mean and what was at stake in the case—after all, how could a minor, innocently intended mistake carry business-destroying penalties?

He hoped a meeting with the plaintiff's lawyer would simply clear it all up, and that they would simply drop the case. He asked me to arrange it. I knew better than to think the meeting would result in the case being dropped, but sometimes lessons are better learned by demonstration.

At the meeting, the attorney on the other side went through the damages calculation and gave a demand number that was even higher than what I'd estimated. (And that was after acknowledging that my client's mistake wasn't done on purpose. Malice wasn't required for this particular claim.)

"How can you live with yourself?" my client shouted, coming out of his chair. Not understanding damages until that moment, he grossly underestimated the case. Besides a little wasted time in an early meeting with the opposing lawyer, it cost him the emotional upset of shock and delayed our defense by several weeks. It wasn't the end of the world, however, and once my client understood the stakes, we were able to agree on a more effective litigation plan.

What the Plaintiff Is Actually Asking For

The damages number in a complaint is not your destiny. In fact, it typically bears little relation to where the case finally ends up in settlement or after a verdict. It is what they are asking for, drafted by an attorney whose job is to frame the claim as favorably as possible for their client. It is not a neutral assessment of what the case is worth, and it is not necessarily what a jury would award even if the plaintiff won on every claim.

Complaints are also sometimes drafted with inflated numbers deliberately—high enough to trigger insurance coverage thresholds, to establish jurisdiction in particular courts, to create psychological pressure on the defendant, to invite media attention, or simply because there is no penalty for asking for more than you can get. The point is, it's not a reliable number for evaluating your exposure and risk.

Your lawyer will help you assess the realistic value of the claims as opposed to the pleaded value. That said, you should not conclude that your case does not involve genuine exposure just because the demand number is likely unreliable. To evaluate what is truly at risk, it is helpful to under the types of damages a plaintiff can seek.

Types of Damages

Compensatory damages are the most common category of damages you'll find in a complaint. And they are just what they sound like: they compensate the plaintiff for actual losses, such as money they lost in a breached contract or lost wages, costs they incurred to fix the harm they suffered, or the value of property that was damaged or destroyed. In a contract dispute, compensatory damages are typically the difference between what the plaintiff was promised and what they received. In a personal injury case, they include medical expenses, lost wages, and similar quantifiable losses.

General damages, sometimes called non-economic damages, cover harms that are real but harder to quantify: pain and suffering, emotional distress, reputational harm, and loss of enjoyment of life. These are the damages that vary most dramatically from case to case and jury to jury, and they are often where the largest and most unpredictable awards occur. A case with modest economic damages can still produce a very large verdict if general damages are in play.

Punitive damages are awarded not to compensate the plaintiff but to punish the defendant for conduct that was egregious. Cases seeking punitive damages will allege fraud, malice, oppression, or reckless disregard for the plaintiffs' rights. Punitive damages are available only in certain types of cases, like intentional torts and fraud. They are also subject to constitutional limits. Punitive awards that are grossly disproportionate to compensatory damages are often reduced by appellate courts and may be unconstitutional. But in cases where they are available and the facts support them, they can be very large.

Statutory damages apply in certain types of cases where a statute sets a specific damages amount per violation, sometimes without requiring the plaintiff to prove actual loss. These are usually fines or penalties, but can also include liquidated damages, treble damages, and disgorgement. Consumer protection statutes, privacy laws, intellectual property claims, and employment laws sometimes include statutory damages provisions. These can multiply quickly in cases involving multiple violations or multiple plaintiffs (like class actions), and they are worth understanding early if your case involves statutory claims.

Interest can also be awarded in cases, both pre- and post-judgment. In cases where there is no interest rate set by a contract, the state may have a set legal interest rate, like a simple ten percent. Since litigation can take years, interest can add up surprisingly fast.

Attorney Fee Awards

In the American legal system, which differs from other countries, each party generally pays their own attorney's fees regardless of who wins. This is called the American Rule, and it is the default in most civil litigation. But there are significant exceptions, and you need to know whether any of them apply to your case.

Modern statutes—particularly in employment law, consumer protection, civil rights, and intellectual property—include fee-shifting provisions that require the losing party to pay the winning party's attorney's fees. If you are being sued under a statute that includes a fee-shifting provision, your exposure is not just the damages the plaintiff claims; it is also whatever their lawyer charges them to prosecute the case, which can be substantial.

Worse for defendants, in most of these statutes, if the defendant wins, he does not similar get attorneys' fees from the plaintiff. The fee shifting is one-sided. And even if the case is low-value (say wages owed that are only a few thousand dollars), the plaintiff's attorney fee is not capped. It can exceed the underlying damages award by six figures.

The traditional way that legal fees get shifted is by contract. If the dispute arises from a contract and that contract contains an attorney fee clause, the winner may be entitled to their fees from the loser. Read the contract at issue in your case and ask your lawyer whether it contains such a provision. In most contracts, fee-shifting also benefits you if you win. Some contracts have one-sided fee-shifting provisions, but many jurisdictions read one-sided prevailing party fee provisions as mutual.

In cases where fee-shifting applies, the litigation math changes dramatically. They create substantial risk for any party subject to a fee award if they lose. They also de-risk strong legal and factual positions. They can be used to leverage a case into settlement, as well. It is no exaggeration to say that attorneys' fees and cost of suit can be the primary factor in driving litigation and settlement amounts, in fact.

Calculating Damages Exposure

I strongly recommend calculating, at least roughly, your damages exposure early in a case. As noted in Part 7, spending $30,000 to defend a $20,000 case makes little economic sense. Higher stakes warrant a more substantial litigation budget. The only way you can know what a case is worth and how to set up a defense is to know your damages exposure.

This is much easier for an experienced lawyer to do than it'll be for you. In the vast majority of cases, I can figure out the rough damages exposure during my initial review of the case.

If you want to work on this, the steps aren't straightforward enough to write into a book. That is because all the different classes of damages turn on facts, the legal theories and laws involved, the statutes of limitations and filing timetables, etcetera. Also, while compensatory damages, statutory damages, and interest are relatively straightforward to calculate, it's nearly impossible to calculate non-economic damages. Along with attorneys' fees and the risk of punitive damages, general damages are something a lawyer would estimate for you based almost entirely on relevant experience.

But you can look at the allegations and figure some things based on information you have. If it's a property damage claim, you might have an idea of fair market repair or replacement. If it's an injury claim, they may have provided a statement of medical expenses and lost wages with the initial papers. If it is an employment dispute, you start with the wages of the employee. If it is a business deal gone bad, start with contract losses.

There's something mercenary about understanding damages first, admittedly. It's not about who is right or who is wrong. But the uncomfortable reality is that few people can afford to litigate for justice. Litigation is nearly always driven by the economics of it. Start getting comfortable with that idea, because if you focus on being right first, you will likely come to regret that decision months or years down the line, even if you ultimately win.

Building a Litigation Budget

Once your lawyer has assessed the claims and your exposure, you should have a direct conversation about the anticipated cost of defense. This conversation is sometimes awkward because neither side has perfect information at the outset, and lawyers can quote you some terrifyingly high numbers. But it is important to discuss it, regardless.

Ask your lawyer for a phased budget—not a single number for the entire case, but estimates broken down by phase: pleadings and initial motions, discovery, pretrial motions, and trial. Each phase has different cost drivers and potential forks and off-ramps in the litigation. The pleadings phase is usually the most predictable. Discovery is the least predictable because its scope depends heavily on what the other side and third parties do and how much everyone fights over evidence. Trial costs are astronomical because they hit at once and require intense, unrelenting work in a relatively short timeframe.

Ask specifically whether the discovery budget includes costs for depositions and experts. As discussed in Step 7, hard costs accrue on top of legal fees. If your case is likely to require expert testimony—which is common in cases involving technical, medical, financial, or professional standards issues—get an early estimate of what that will cost and factor it into your budget.

Ask about the relationship between the litigation budget and the damages at stake. A competent lawyer will help you think about this honestly. If the cost of a full defense through trial approaches or exceeds your realistic exposure, that changes how you should think about defense strategy and settlement. Conversely, if the plaintiff's demand is wildly disproportionate to their actual damages, knowing that helps you resist pressure to settle for more than the case is worth. **Sometimes the value of a good defense is how much it saves you in settlement**.

The Cost-Benefit Framework

Litigation is not just a legal problem. It isn't just a testing of law and evidence in pursuit of justice. I know that's a cynical statement, but is categorically true.

Litigation is driven almost entirely by financial decisions, both yours and the other parties'. Every step of the litigation process has a cost, and that cost should be evaluated against the realistic outcome range your lawyer can help you identify.

This does not mean you should always settle to avoid costs. Sometimes the right answer is to fight, because the exposure is real and a negotiated resolution is not available on reasonable terms, or because the case involves something—a business relationship, a reputation, a principle—that has value beyond the financial calculation. But those decisions should be made consciously, with full information about what they cost, not by default.

The framework needed to evaluate the economics of a case is simple. What is my realistic exposure if I lose? What does it cost to get through each stage of the litigation? What is the probability of winning or settling at each stage, and how do those numbers compare to what it would cost to resolve the case now? While the answers usually are not easy to hear or nail down with certainty, your lawyer can give you informed estimates and educate you on where things get truly murky. The resulting risk analysis is the foundation of every intelligent litigation decision you will make.

STEP EIGHT EXECUTIVE SUMMARY

- The damages number in the complaint usually has little resemblance to the actual stakes of the case.

- Educate yourself on the types of damages at issue: compensatory, general, punitive, and statutory. Each has different exposure and different predictability.

- Punitive damages are available only in cases involving egregious conduct. While rare, they can be enormous sums when awarded.

- Understand whether your case involves fee-shifting requiring the loser to pay the winner's attorney's fees, and whether they are one-way for plaintiffs only. The availability of attorney's fees can take over and drive the litigation entirely.

- Ask your lawyer for a phased litigation budget, not just a single number. Understand the cost drivers at each stage.

- Evaluate litigation as a financial decision. The cost of defense at each stage should be weighed against your realistic exposure and the probability of various outcomes.

- This analysis is the foundation of every intelligent decision you will make about how aggressively to fight and when to consider settlement.

STEP 9

CONSIDER EARLY SETTLEMENT

Nobody wants to settle. At least, not at first.

When a lawsuit lands on your desk, settlement feels like surrender to a pirate—like paying someone who wronged you, admitting to something you did not do, or rewarding abusive behavior with a check. The anger that most defendants feel in the first days after being served makes the idea of resolution feel like defeat.

I understand that feeling. I have felt it myself. And I am here to tell you it is one of the most expensive feelings you will ever indulge. If you choose not to write a check immediately—and many times that is not the course I advise—know why you are doing it.

It's the Principle of the Thing

As the lawyer, it is not my job to force a client to settle if they don't want to. I'm no shrinking violet, and if you want me to play in court, I usually will enjoy it. But I will still strongly urge clients to settle when it's economically more favorable, as that's almost always what's best for them.

In the vast majority of cases, at the outset, I will hear something like, "I want to fight. It's the principle of the thing." The problem is, sometimes the client means it only until we are a year and tens of thousands into a litigation. Then they hit their limit, want out, and everything we'd done ends up being wasted time and money.

I had a case once where a customer sued for a refund on a contract. The defendant had performed, and the customer was not entitled to a refund. An attorney's fee provision made the customer on the hook if he lost. But the plaintiff wasn't collectible, and the judgment was worthless. Winning was a Pyrrhic victory, and everyone was unhappy in the end—including me because the client didn't want to pay his bill.

If it really is the principle for you, then understand that you are spending money for a moral or personal position, and be at peace with that. Justice is a luxury that most of us can't afford.

Why Settlement Is Not Surrender

Settlement is not an admission of liability. Settlement agreements almost universally include language stating that payment is not an admission of wrongdoing. Courts routinely instruct juries they may not draw any inference from the fact that a party settled a related claim. The law treats a settlement as a practical resolution of a dispute, not a confession.

More importantly, settlement is how the overwhelming majority of civil lawsuits end. As discussed in Step 6, only about one percent of civil cases go to trial through verdict. The other ninety-nine percent settle before trial, during trial, after summary judgment, sometimes even after trial. Settlement is not the exception in civil litigation. It is the norm. With rare exceptions, the question is not whether your case will settle, but when and on what terms.

The timing of that settlement matters enormously. Cases that settle early cost a fraction of what cases cost when they settle late. The legal fees and hard costs you save by resolving a case at the pleadings stage versus after two years of litigation can easily run into six figures. Early settlement is not just emotionally easier. It is financially rational.

That said, settlement is a negotiation, and there are several emotional and economic factors that drive it. Sometimes later settlement will be the better course, after you use litigation tools to narrow the scope or cause the other side enough pain to be reasonable. In situations like that, a later settlement will be the better economic choice.

What Drives Settlement Value

Settlement value is not the same as case value. Case value is what a jury might award if the plaintiff won at trial. Settlement value is what the case is worth to resolve right now, accounting for the cost and uncertainty of getting to that trial verdict.

Several factors drive settlement value:

Liability risk. How strong is the plaintiff's case on the merits? A plaintiff with a compelling theory of liability and powerful evidence commands a higher settlement value than one with a weak case. Your lawyer's honest assessment of liability risk is the starting point for any settlement analysis.

Damages risk. Even if liability is clear, the range of possible damages outcomes affects settlement value. A case where the plaintiff might recover anywhere from $50,000 to $500,000, depending on the jury, has a different settlement calculus than one where damages are fixed and predictable. Similarly, things like fee shifting can add or remove risk.

Cost of litigation. The expense to litigate the case impacts the settlement value. On the defense side, even a defendant who is likely to win must weigh the cost of winning against the cost of resolving. This is the nuisance-value dynamic discussed in Step 6. Similarly, a plaintiff with a weak case who is facing a protracted battle may settle for significantly less than their case is nominally worth. If the plaintiff's lawyer is litigating on a contingency fee, he will want to invest as little as necessary while maximizing results, and the defense can exploit that.

Business and personal considerations. Litigation has costs beyond the financial. It consumes management time and attention, creates reputational risk, stresses relationships, and generates uncertainty that can affect business operations and planning. A settlement that looks expensive in pure dollars may be rational when those non-financial costs are factored in. And, honestly, there's a real value to "buying the peace." Life is too short to engage too often in conflict.

The plaintiff's situation. Plaintiffs have their own financial pressures and risk tolerances. A plaintiff who is funding their own litigation and has limited resources may be more motivated to settle than one with more resources. Emotions also play into it substantially. A plaintiff may feel strongly that they want vindication of their wrong. They want justice, or vengeance. Conversely, a plaintiff may find the litigation emotionally intolerable and be willing to drop the case relatively quickly. Their family and lawyers will influence their decisions. And sometimes you simply have to educate the other side about the weaknesses of their case so that they will arrive at a more palatable number.

The Mechanics of Settlement

Settlement can happen informally, through a direct exchange of offers between lawyers, or through a structured process. The most common structured process is mediation (sometimes called a settlement conference or conciliation).

Mediation is a negotiation facilitated by a neutral third party, the mediator, who has no power to impose a result but helps the parties find common ground. Mediators are typically experienced lawyers or retired judges with expertise in the relevant area of law. The process is *strictly* confidential. Nothing said in mediation can be used in court, and the mediator cannot share information with the other side or outside of the mediation without the express permission of the revealing party, which allows both sides to speak more candidly about the weaknesses of their case and their actual settlement range than they would in open litigation.

Many courts require the parties to attempt mediation before trial. But mediation can happen at any stage of the litigation, and the earlier it happens, the cheaper it is. That said, many lawyers will not want to mediate a case until after significant discovery is completed so that they can evaluate the case with more certainty.

Some cases settle in mediation on the first attempt. Others require multiple sessions. Some do not settle in mediation at all, but settle afterwards on the foundation the mediator built. And sometimes mediation fails. That said, in my personal experience, mediation has a very high success rate and will usually resolve the case once everyone is in the right financial and emotional space to compromise.

Your lawyer will prepare you for mediation by walking you through your realistic case evaluation, your settlement range—the range between the minimum you would accept and the maximum you would pay—and the strategy for the negotiation. Go into mediation prepared to negotiate seriously, not to perform outrage. The mediator has seen every variety of righteous indignation and is not moved by it. What moves mediation toward resolution is a realistic assessment of risk on both sides and a willingness to find a number that both parties can live with.

As many cases as I've seen settle through mediation, lawyers are also perfectly capable of settling cases between them, and will to avoid the cost of mediation (which can be several thousand dollars).

When to Push for Early Settlement

This book is about what to do at the outset of the case, and that includes seriously considering early settlement so that you are not in the lawsuit for months or years. Early settlement makes the most sense when one or more of the following is true:

The liability risk is real. If your lawyer's honest assessment is that the plaintiff has a strong case on the merits, the cost of fighting to a likely loss is almost always higher than the cost of resolving early. Pride is an expensive litigation strategy.

The cost of defense is disproportionate to the stakes. If fully defending the case would cost more than the realistic damages exposure, resolution on any reasonable terms is financially rational, even if you believe you would win. One time, I settled a case in mediation that was brought against my firm by a vendor who didn't fully perform (it was small claims, and the mediation was free) because it was simply too ridiculous to spend money fighting over $500. I follow my own economic advice!

The case involves sensitive information. Discovery is a remarkably effective tool for publicly exposing information you would prefer to keep private, such as financial records, embarrassing emails and texts, personnel files, personal relationships, medical and emotional issues, and business procedures. If the litigation is likely to expose things that are embarrassing, competitively sensitive, or damaging to relationships, early settlement keeps those things out of the public record.

The disruption to your business or personal life is significant. Some defendants find that the ongoing uncertainty and management distraction of litigation costs them more in operational terms than the settlement would. That is a legitimate consideration.

When Not to Settle Early

Early settlement is not always the right answer. There are cases worth fighting.

If the plaintiff's case is weak, and their demand is unreasonable, fighting sends a message. You are testing resolve, and it can be highly effective. The message to the plaintiff and their lawyer, and to anyone else who might consider bringing a similar claim, is that you are not an easy target. A reputation for aggressive defense deters future nuisance litigation.

Similarly, if the plaintiff is acting in bad faith—using litigation as a harassment tool, making demands that bear no relationship to any legitimate claim—giving them money rewards the behavior and may invite more of it. Sometimes it is as simple as the plaintiff and her lawyer having misconceptions about the law. I frequently teach the other side the meaning of FAFO—they pick a stupid fight and then they learn that was a bad plan.

Finally, if the case involves a principle that matters to you or your business, settling may create precedent or waiver problems that cost you more in the long run than the litigation itself. For example, if you do not defend certain rights in one instance, you may lose them across all instances. This is the case in intellectual property, because if you do not protect it, then it looks like you've abandoned your ownership claim on it.

Your lawyer will help you assess which situation you are in. The key is that the decision should be made deliberately, with a full understanding of the costs and risks on both sides, not driven by anger on one end or panic on the other.

Settlement Is a Negotiation, Not a Capitulation

I already said this, but it bears repeating.

Your case is likely to settle at some point. Be intentional about when and how, and don't see it as waving a white flag of surrender or admitting wrongdoing. And if you choose to die on a hill, do it with zeal so you have no regrets later.

STEP NINE EXECUTIVE SUMMARY

- Settlement is not an admission of liability. It is a practical resolution of a dispute that the law treats as exactly that.

- Ninety-nine percent of civil cases settle. The question is usually when and on what terms.

- Early settlement can save you money. Cases that resolve before significant discovery cost a fraction of what cases cost when they settle after years of litigation, but the plaintiff needs to cooperate.

- Settlement value is driven by liability risk, damages risk, cost of defense, business disruption, and the plaintiff's own financial and emotional situation and risk tolerance.

- Mediation is a common settlement mechanism. Go in prepared with a realistic case evaluation and a settlement range, not a performance of outrage.

- Some cases are definitely worth fighting, at least to some degree. Make that decision deliberately, not out of anger.

STEP 10

Plan Your finances, upcoming transactions, and assets carefully.

By the time you reach this step, you have done the hard work. You have preserved your evidence, found your lawyer, tendered your insurance, and have a more concrete idea of what you are facing.

But now that you have some rough estimates of cost and settlement postures, a new impulse arises: hiding assets or using protected assets to settle.

The anxiety of a lawsuit sometimes prompts financial decisions that feel protective and rational in the moment, but are anything but. Moving money. Transferring property. Restructuring your business. Gifting assets to family members. These actions, taken after a lawsuit is filed—or even after litigation becomes reasonably foreseeable—can expose you to consequences far worse than the original lawsuit. They can transform a civil dispute into something that looks like fraud.

Do not make financial moves without talking to your lawyer

first. That is the entire message of this chapter, and everything that follows explains why.

Blowing Up Your Financial Future Accidentally

I have two stories for you. The first is a client who was hit with tens of thousands in medical bills after a catastrophic illness. After they had exhausted their savings, they fell behind and ended up in collections.

Their next move: cashing out their 401k to pay off some of the collection suits. But that wasn't enough. The bills, and the collections, continued, and they ended up in bankruptcy. In bankruptcy, the bills were negotiated for pennies on the dollar and they emerged debt-free.

But they also emerged depleted of retirement savings. Which was sad because in bankruptcy, their 401k was an exempt asset that they didn't have to use toward paying down debts. In other words, they could've kept that money for themselves while still handling all the creditors in the bankruptcy process. Because if medical bills are going to bankrupt you—and its the most common cause of bankruptcy—you might as well come out of such a horrible ordeal as best as you can.

Here is my second story: I once had a client transfer his business to his brother before the lawsuit was filed, thinking that would protect the business. He was retiring anyway and planned to give the business to his brother, who already worked in the business. And he didn't want the business to take a financial hit and be forced to lay off employees he'd had for decades. So his intentions were good, but the result was that his brother was also sued, and the assets were reached, anyway. And he looked like a dishonest person to the judge, impacting the entire case and making defense harder.

What Is a Fraudulent Transfer?

My second story illustrates a fraudulent transfer. A fraudulent transfer—also sometimes called a fraudulent conveyance—is a transfer of assets made intending to hinder, delay, or defraud creditors. Every state has a version of the Uniform Fraudulent Transfer Act or its successor, the Uniform Voidable Transactions Act, and federal bankruptcy law contains similar provisions. These laws give courts the power to unwind asset transfers—to reverse them, as if they never happened—and to impose additional sanctions on the parties involved, as warranted.

You do not have to intend to defraud anyone for a transfer to be challenged as fraudulent. Courts also recognize what is called constructive fraud. Those are transfers made without adequate consideration (meaning you gave something away for less than it was worth) at a time when you were insolvent or became insolvent as a result. Intent is not required for constructive fraud. The transfer itself, under the circumstances, is enough.

The timing of a transfer matters enormously. A transfer made after a lawsuit is filed, or after litigation becomes reasonably foreseeable, is scrutinized much more heavily than one made years before any dispute arose. Courts look at any circumstances that suggest a transfer was motivated by a desire to put assets beyond a creditor's reach. These include transfers to family members or insiders, transfers for little or no consideration, transfers of substantially all of a debtor's assets, and transfers made shortly after a lawsuit was filed or a significant debt was incurred.

If a court finds that a transfer was fraudulent, it can void the transfer entirely. The plaintiff can then pursue it, sometimes with attachments even before a judgment has been entered in the case! In cases of actual fraud, courts can also impose punitive damages and, in some jurisdictions, refer the matter for criminal prosecution. And both of those things do happen.

Common Mistakes Defendants Make

Transferring assets to family members. This is the most common mistake, and the one courts are most suspicious of. Putting your house in your spouse's name, gifting money to your children, transferring business interests to a sibling, when done after a lawsuit is filed or becomes foreseeable, are classic examples of fraudulent transfer. That your family member received the asset in good faith and had nothing to do with the lawsuit does not protect them from being added to the lawsuit as a defendant.

Moving money offshore. Transferring funds to foreign bank accounts after being sued is not a sophisticated asset protection strategy, despite what some internet sources will tell you. It is a red flag that triggers aggressive collection efforts, potential contempt proceedings, and in some cases criminal referrals. Courts have broad powers to compel the return of assets moved offshore to avoid judgment. Courts (especially family courts) will jail people who do not repatriate assets until they do.

Filing for bankruptcy impulsively. Bankruptcy can be a legitimate and powerful tool in the right circumstances, but filing for bankruptcy in response to a lawsuit is often unnecessary and has its own financial consequences. Besides impacting all your assets and credit before the outcome of the litigation is certain, bankruptcy requires complete disclosure of all assets, all transfers, and all financial activity for a significant lookback period. Transfers made before a bankruptcy filing are scrutinized intensively by the bankruptcy trustee, and fraudulent transfers discovered in bankruptcy can result in denial of discharge—meaning you do not get the fresh start bankruptcy is supposed to provide.

Intermingling personal and business assets. If you operate through a corporation or LLC, one of the most important protections that entity provides is the separation of your personal assets from your business liabilities. That protection is called the corporate veil, and it depends entirely on maintaining a genuine separation between personal and business finances. If you have been paying personal expenses from a business account, commingling funds, or treating the business as a personal piggy bank, a plaintiff can argue that the corporate veil should be pierced. When the veil is pierced, that means the plaintiff can go after your personal assets for a business debt. Intermingling is a *common mistake* by small business owners. Talk to your lawyer about it.

Moving assets from exempt to non-exempt status. Every state has exemption laws that protect certain assets from creditor claims. For example, a homestead exemption protects some equity in your primary residence. There are exemptions for retirement accounts, tools of the trade, vehicles, personal property, and certain types of income and jointly held property. These exemptions can be significant, and they are worth understanding. If you have significant assets, use good planning before any dispute arises to exempt and protect as many of your assets as you can. And please, I'm begging you, do not change how you hold your assets or make any financial moves (like cashing out retirement accounts or selling your house) until after you speak with an attorney about the consequences.

Accelerating or restructuring major transactions. If you have a significant business or financial transactions in progress—an acquisition, a real estate deal, a major contract or investment—a pending lawsuit affects how that transaction should be structured and documented. Rushing to close a transaction before a judgment can attach, or restructuring a deal in a way that reduces your apparent net worth, can create fraudulent transfer exposure and complicate both the litigation and the transaction. Neither your litigation lawyer nor your transactional lawyer should be operating in isolation on these matters.

What You Should Do Instead

Talk to your lawyer before you move anything. This is not a situation where it is easier to ask forgiveness than permission. Fraudulent transfer liability is much easier to create than to undo, and the consequences of getting it wrong extend well beyond the original lawsuit.

That conversation should cover your current asset picture: what you own, how it is titled, what is encumbered and what is not, and any transactions or financial moves you are considering. Your lawyer may involve a financial advisor, a tax professional, or a bankruptcy attorney depending on what is at stake.

There are legitimate asset protection strategies that can be employed even after a lawsuit is filed, but they are narrow, fact-specific, and require careful legal guidance to execute without creating new problems. Do not attempt them without counsel.

The fundamental principle is this: the time to do asset protection planning is before you need it. Once a lawsuit is filed, your options narrow dramatically. What you can do is make sure you do not make things worse, and the single most effective way to do that is to stop, breathe, and call your lawyer before you sign anything, transfer anything, move anything, or make any major financial decisions.

STEP TEN EXECUTIVE SUMMARY

- A lawsuit creates powerful and dangerous impulses to move, hide, cash out, or protect assets. Resist all of them until you have spoken with your lawyer.

- Fraudulent transfer laws allow courts to unwind asset transfers made to hinder, delay, or defraud creditors. Even transfers made without fraudulent intent, if they were made for less than fair value while you were insolvent.

- Timing matters. Transfers made after a lawsuit is filed or becomes foreseeable are scrutinized heavily and carry significant risk.

- Do not transfer assets to family members, move money offshore, or restructure your business in response to a lawsuit without legal guidance.

- Do not file for bankruptcy impulsively. It has consequences and can be premature early in litigation. Bankruptcy also requires full disclosure of all assets and prior transfers. Fraudulent transfers discovered in bankruptcy can cause denial of discharge.

- Maintain strict separation between personal and business finances. Intermingling gives plaintiffs grounds to pierce the corporate veil and reach your personal assets.

- Do not move assets from exempt to non-exempt categories after a lawsuit is filed without counsel. You are adding risk unnecessarily.

- If you have major transactions in progress, make sure your litigation lawyer and your transactional lawyer are communicating. Do not let a pending lawsuit and a pending deal proceed in isolation.

- The time for asset protection planning is before you need it. After a lawsuit is filed, your options narrow. Your job now is to avoid making things worse.

- Before you sign anything, transfer anything, or move anything, **call your lawyer**!

BONUS CHAPTER

The Risks of Relying on AI Instead of Counsel

Every week, I see the consequences of a decision that is becoming more common and more costly: someone got sued, panicked, and turned to an AI chatbot for legal advice before (or instead of) hiring a lawyer.

I understand why. AI tools are free, available at three in the morning, non-judgmental, and fluent in the language of confidence. They produce answers that look authoritative. They cite cases, explain statutes, and walk you through procedures in calm, organized prose. If you are frightened and looking for reassurance, an AI will give it to you—clearly, immediately, and completely without the professional accountability that makes legal advice worth having.

That is precisely the problem.

What AI Does Well, and What It Does Not

Let me be clear about something before I explain why AI is dangerous in legal situations: AI tools are genuinely useful for many things. Research. Summarization. Drafting starting points. Understanding general legal concepts. Translating dense statutory language into plain English. If you want to understand what a motion to dismiss generally is, or what the elements of a breach of contract claim typically include, an AI can give you a reasonable orientation.

What AI cannot do is practice law. And the distinction between general legal information and legal advice specific to your situation is not a technicality. It is the entire difference between something useful and something dangerous.

Legal advice requires judgment: the application of law to specific facts in a specific jurisdiction before a specific judge, shaped by local court customs, recent case law, the particular tendencies of opposing counsel, and dozens of other variables that no AI model has access to or can reliably assess. Legal advice requires accountability: a licensed professional whose livelihood, reputation, and bar license depend on the quality of the guidance they give you. Legal advice requires a relationship: the attorney-client privilege that protects your communications and allows you to speak candidly without fear that your words will be used against you.

AI provides none of those things. It provides information. Information and advice are not the same thing, and in a lawsuit, confusing them can be catastrophic.

The Hallucination Problem

AI language models generate text by predicting which words are likely to follow other words, based on patterns in their training data. They do not look things up. They do not verify. They do not know when they are wrong. And they are wrong with alarming frequency on legal matters. But you won't know because they are confidently, fluently wrong; and wrong in ways that are difficult for a non-lawyer to detect.

The most dangerous manifestation of this is what the AI industry calls hallucination: the generation of plausible-sounding but entirely fabricated information. In legal contexts, this most commonly takes the form of fake case citations. An astounding number of litigants have now been sanctioned for citing cases that do not exist, decided by courts that never heard them, standing for propositions that no court has ever articulated. The sanctions go against not only attorneys but also litigants representing themselves. Hallucinated citations are a big, fat, giant no-no.

In 2023, a New York federal court sanctioned attorneys Steven Schwartz and Peter LoDuca of the firm Levidow, Levidow & Oberman after they submitted a legal brief containing citations to at least six cases that did not exist—all generated by ChatGPT, which the filing attorney had used for research without verifying the citations. The cases had names, docket numbers, courts, and dates, so they looked real. But none of them were real. When the court ordered the attorneys to produce the cases, they could not, because the cases did not exist. The court fined the attorneys $5,000 each and referred the matter for potential additional disciplinary proceedings.

That case, *Mata v. Avianca*, became a landmark warning about AI in legal practice and generated extensive coverage and commentary in the legal profession. It was not an isolated incident. Similar cases have followed in jurisdictions across the country, involving both represented parties and self-represented litigants who used AI to prepare their own filings. And the sanctions are getting larger the longer this goes on; the courts are fed up.

For a defendant who relies on AI to understand their case, draft their own response, or evaluate their legal options, the hallucination risk is acute. You may be making decisions based on law that does not exist, cases that were never decided, or rules that apply in a different jurisdiction or have been superseded. You will not know the difference, because the AI will not tell you.

The Confidentiality Problem

In Step 1 of this book, I told you that almost everything you share outside the attorney-client relationship is potentially discoverable. That warning applies with particular force to AI tools.

When you type the facts of your lawsuit into a chatbot, you are not communicating with a lawyer. You are inputting data into a software platform operated by a technology company. That conversation is not protected by attorney-client privilege. Depending on the platform's terms of service and data practices, it may be stored, analyzed, used to train future models, or disclosed in response to legal process.

This creates two problems. First, you have now disclosed your case information to a non-lawyer, so it is discoverable. And because it is discoverable, you now also have a duty to preserve it. Deleting your chats is no prohibited!

Major AI platforms have faced litigation and regulatory scrutiny over their data practices, and the legal landscape around AI-generated content and data retention is still developing. What is clear is that no AI platform provides anything resembling the confidentiality protections of the attorney-client relationship. When you tell ChatGPT that your former employee is suing you for discrimination and here are the facts, you have created a discoverable record of that disclosure. The opposing party can force you to provide it, and may also subpoena OpenAI for the backups to make sure you aren't omitting anything.

Courts have already begun grappling with questions about the discoverability of AI-assisted work product, the extent to which AI-generated content can be protected by attorney work product doctrine, and the obligations of lawyers and parties to disclose their use of AI in litigation. The law in this area is developing rapidly and inconsistently across jurisdictions, but the trend is toward greater scrutiny and greater disclosure obligations, not less.

The practical advice is the same as it was in Step 1: do not put the facts of your lawsuit into any platform that is not protected by privilege. That includes AI chatbots, social media, search engines, and any other tool operated by a third party. The attorney-client relationship is the only protection the law provides for candid communication about your legal situation. Use it.

The Unauthorized Practice of Law Problem

Every state prohibits the unauthorized practice of law. That is the provision of legal services by someone who is not licensed to practice in that jurisdiction. The prohibition exists to protect the public from unqualified advice on matters where the consequences of error can be severe.

AI tools are not licensed to practice law anywhere. They are not subject to bar oversight, disciplinary proceedings, or malpractice liability. When an AI tells you how to respond to a lawsuit, what defenses to assert, or whether you have a strong case, it is doing something that a human being would be prohibited from doing without a law license. Worse, it is doing so without the accountability structures that make licensure meaningful.

Several state bar associations have issued formal opinions on the use of AI in legal practice, and the trend is consistent: AI can be a tool to assist lawyers, but it cannot substitute for the professional judgment of a licensed attorney. The Florida Bar, the California State Bar, and the American Bar Association, among others, have all issued guidance emphasizing that lawyers remain fully responsible for AI-generated work product and must review and verify everything AI produces before submitting it in any legal proceeding.

For non-lawyers, the implications are starker. Using AI to prepare legal filings, draft responses to complaints, or navigate court procedures is functionally the unauthorized practice of law—not just by the AI company, but potentially by the person using it to substitute for licensed counsel, especially if you are getting help from friends, family members, or paralegals. Courts have sanctioned pro se litigants who submit AI-generated filings containing fabricated citations or legal arguments that reflect a misunderstanding of applicable law.

The Judgment Problem

Beyond the technical failures—hallucinations, confidentiality gaps, regulatory issues—there is a more fundamental problem with relying on AI for legal guidance: AI does not have judgment.

Judgment is the ability to assess a situation in its full complexity, weigh competing considerations, anticipate how a human decision-maker will respond, and choose a course of action that serves your actual interests rather than a generic approximation of them. It is what separates a lawyer who has tried fifty cases from a database of legal information. It is what allows a skilled negotiator to read a mediation and know when to push and when to concede. It is what makes the difference between a motion that wins and a motion that loses, when both are technically competent.

AI is trained on patterns in text. It optimizes for producing output that resembles correct answers. It has no skin in the game, no professional reputation at stake, no understanding of what it actually means for you to lose this lawsuit, and, most importantly, *no humanity*. It cannot sit across a table from opposing counsel and read the room. It cannot appear before a judge who is running out of patience and calibrate accordingly. It cannot look you in the eye and tell you that your instinct about this case is wrong.

The best lawyers bring something to their work that is irreducibly human: the accumulated weight of experience, the ability to connect with other humans in high-stakes situations, and the courage to tell clients things they do not want to hear. None of that is in the training data.

Relying on AI for advice can absolutely steer you wrong. AI can tell you a strategy is a winner when it's not. There are now a growing number of cases where AI has convinced people to fire their lawyers and follow the AI's legal advice, resulting in catastrophic results in the case.

PLEASE DO NOT SUBSTITUTE AI FOR A LAWYER. That is not because lawyers want to protect their jobs. That is because AI is risky and inferior compared to an experienced practitioner, and we all know it. But AI won't tell you that.

What the Courts Are Saying

The judiciary has moved quickly to address AI in litigation, and the direction is clear. Multiple federal courts have adopted local rules requiring disclosure of AI use in legal filings. Some require attorneys to certify that they have reviewed and verified any AI-generated content. Others prohibit AI-generated citations entirely unless independently verified.

In *Mata v. Avianca*, the judge wrote that the attorneys' conduct "reflects a failure to follow through on the straightforward obligation of not misrepresenting the law to the court." He was not sympathetic to the explanation that ChatGPT had generated the fabrications. The professional obligation to verify belonged to the lawyers, not the software. The obligation to verify citations has always existed, by the way, and AI does not change that.

Courts have also begun sanctioning unrepresented individuals for submitting AI-generated filings that contain fabricated citations or misrepresent applicable law. In several cases, courts have struck AI-generated filings entirely, and sometimes dismissed the cases outright.

The message from the judiciary is consistent: AI is not a substitute for legal knowledge, professional judgment, or the duty of candor to the court. The responsibility for what gets filed belongs to the person who files it, regardless of what tool generated the content.

A Practical Note on AI-Assisted Lawyers

It would be misleading to suggest that AI has no role in competent legal practice. Many lawyers, including careful and skilled ones, use AI tools to assist with research, document review, drafting, and analysis. Some versions of these tools have existed a long time in specialized legal research databases like Westlaw and Lexis, and technically spellcheck is a rudimentary AI. When used correctly, AI can improve efficiency without sacrificing quality.

The key phrase is *used correctly*. A lawyer who uses AI as a starting point and then brings their own expertise, verification, and judgment to the work is doing something fundamentally different from a non-lawyer who uses AI as a substitute for hiring counsel. The former is a professional using a tool. The latter is someone trying to replace a professional with a tool. And the consequences of that substitution, in a legal context, fall entirely on the person who made it.

When you are interviewing lawyers, it is entirely appropriate to ask how they use AI in their practice and what their verification process is for AI-generated content. A lawyer who uses AI thoughtfully and transparently is not a red flag. A lawyer who submits AI-generated work product without review is not a responsible professional, and the cases above illustrate what that can cost a client.

The Bottom Line

You are facing a lawsuit. The stakes are real. The process is complicated. The other side has a lawyer whose job is to win.

AI can help you understand general concepts. It can help you prepare questions for your lawyer. It can help you understand a document in plain English. Use it for those things if you find it helpful.

To ensure you do not create discoverable information on your legal strategies and theories, do not use AI to evaluate your case or draft legal filings. Do not run your attorneys' correspondence and documents through an AI because that destroys the privilege. Do not use AI as a substitute for the advice of a licensed attorney who knows your jurisdiction, your facts, and your goals.

The confidentiality you surrender, the fabrications you may not catch, and the judgment you cannot replace are not risks worth taking. You will make your situation worse, and the other side of the case will be switched on enough to catch you at it.

BONUS CHAPTER EXECUTIVE SUMMARY

- AI tools can provide general legal information. They cannot provide legal advice, such as the application of law to your specific facts by a licensed, accountable professional.

- AI hallucinates. It generates fabricated case citations, invented legal standards, and confident misinformation that is difficult for non-lawyers to detect. Courts have sanctioned attorneys and non-represented litigants for submitting AI-generated filings containing fake citations and unsupported legal theories.

- Anything you type into an AI chatbot is not protected by attorney-client privilege and may be discoverable. Do not input the facts of your lawsuit into any platform not protected by privilege.

- AI is not licensed to practice law. Using it to substitute for licensed counsel may expose you to sanctions and leaves you without any professional accountability or malpractice protection if the advice is wrong.

- AI does not have judgment. That requires the accumulated experience, human insight, and professional courage that distinguishes a skilled lawyer from a database of legal text.

- Courts are moving quickly to regulate AI in litigation. Multiple federal courts now require disclosure of AI use and verification of AI-generated content. Sanctions for unverified AI filings are increasing.

- Do not put your lawyer's papers and communications into AI because that destroys the privilege and it'll get subpoenaed.

- The responsibility for what gets filed and argued in court rests on the people in court, not the software they used.

AI is a tool, and it is best used by your lawyer to create efficient representation, instead of you.

POSTSCRIPT

Do you need to contact me?

If you would like to contact me about this book, any of my other books, or even just to say hi, follow this link and fill out my contact form. Please do not include confidential information about your legal issues. Contacting me does not create an attorney-client relationship. You can also contact me through my websites below.

About the Author

Alicia I. Dearn, Esq. works as a trial lawyer, entrepreneur, and author. She publishes on topics of law, business, politics, and memoir. "Amelia Elliot" is the pen name for Ms. Dearn's fictional works in women's and literary fiction, romance, sci-fi, and political and legal thrillers. She lives with her husband, three big dogs, and three riotous kittens.

AliciaDearn.com

NoAIJustExperience.com

Did this book help you? Leave a review!

Please support independent authors and small publishers by leaving ratings and reviews with the retailers of purchase. It's one of the best ways to thank and support independent creatives. **Your positive feedback means the world to me.**

www.ingramcontent.com/pod-product-compliance
Lightning Source LLC
LaVergne TN
LVHW010925110826
845149LV00013B/2480

* 9 7 8 1 9 6 5 2 8 2 0 6 9 *